1218–50

COMBAT

Templar Knight
VERSUS
Mamluk Warrior

David Campbell

OSPREY PUBLISHING
Bloomsbury Publishing Plc

Kemp House, Chawley Park, Cumnor Hill, Oxford OX2 9PH, UK
29 Earlsfort Terrace, Dublin 2, Ireland
1385 Broadway, 5th Floor, New York, NY 10018, USA
Email: info@ospreypublishing.com
www.ospreypublishing.com

OSPREY is a trademark of Osprey Publishing Ltd

First published in Great Britain in 2015

A catalogue record for this book is available from the British Library

Print ISBN: 978 1 4728 1333 6
ePDF: 978 1 4728 1334 3
ePub: 978 1 4728 1335 0

Index by Rob Munro
Maps and diagrams by www.bounford.com
Typeset in Univers, Sabon and Adobe Garamond Pro
Originated by PDQ Media, Bungay, UK
Printed and bound in India by Replika Press Private Ltd.

MIX
Paper from responsible sources
FSC® C016779
www.fsc.org

23 24 25 26 27   10 9 8 7 6 5 4

The Woodland Trust
Osprey Publishing supports the Woodland Trust, the UK's leading woodland conservation charity.

Author's dedication
This book is dedicated to Geoff Banks, in the faint hope that such an honour might encourage him to actually read the text rather than just look at the pictures.

Author's acknowledgements
I would like to thank the following: the Verger and staff of Temple Church, London for their kind permission to photograph the effigies contained therein; Dr David Nicolle, for his advice and kind permission to use some of his original photography; David Greentree, without whom I would not have gone down this particular path; Graham Campbell, for paying the bills among other things; Rick Lippiett, for his useful advice and contacts; Geoff Banks, for a miscellany of exceedingly small but nevertheless useful tasks; Gökmen Altinkulp, whose practical knowledge of Turkish horse-archery traditions and equestrianism proved both insightful and a material aid in the writing of this book; Lukas Novotny of the Saluki Bow Company (www.salukibow.com), for his generous help in answering questions and providing images; the staff of Southsea Library; the British Library (http://www.bl.uk/catalogues/illuminatedmanuscripts/welcome.htm); the Metropolitan Museum of Art in New York (http://www.metmuseum.org/), who, through their OASC (Open Access for Scholarly Content) system have made a broad range of images of artworks widely and freely available for scholarly and academic publication; and finally to my editor Nick Reynolds, whose attention to detail always makes for a better book, and for his impressive reserves of patience.

Editor's note
Though the *mamālik* were Turkic in origin and language, the literature that surrounds them is mostly written in Arabic, and thus the military terms, names of weapons and of armour are given in that tongue. Measurements are given in imperial throughout. For ease of comparison please refer to the following conversion table:

1 mile = 1.6km
1yd = 0.9m
1ft = 0.3m
1in = 2.54cm/25.4mm
1lb = 0.45kg

www.ospreypublishing.com
To find out more about our authors and books visit our website. Here you will find extracts, author interviews, details of forthcoming events and the option to sign-up for our newsletter.

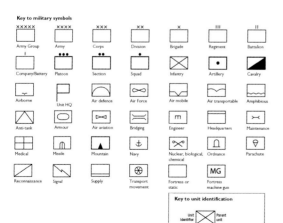

CONTENTS

Introduction

Salāh ad-Dīn had come so close. Building on the successes of his predecessor Nūr ad-Dīn, *atābak* of Aleppo (r. 1146–74), Salāh ad-Dīn became the personification of the resurgent Islamic states of the region, bringing a vigour and consistency to the war against the Franks that bore much fruit; he unified the Muslim lands that surrounded their kingdoms, he eroded their possessions, took their strongholds and, at Hattin in 1187, destroyed much of their military capability for a generation. His immediate failure, due in part to the tenacity of his Frankish enemies and their vital reinforcement by the Third Crusade (1189–92), may not have been the end of the story had he not died in 1193. Even so, the world he left behind seemed an ominously threatening one to the Crusader States, beset as they were on all sides by an enemy that had been in the ascendant for decades, and had nearly driven them into the sea. However, it was Salāh ad-Dīn, his personality, his authority, and his vision that had shaped and driven that ascendancy, and without his guiding hand drawing together the political and military strength of the region's fractious princes, much would change.

Lost lands and the fall of Jerusalem dug sharp spurs into the West, revitalizing the crusading movement and driving the ambitious

Salāh ad-Dīn ravaging the Holy Land. Such depredations reduced the Latin states' lands to little more than a series of cities and outposts along the Syrian coastline. (© The British Library Board, Yates Thompson 12 f. 161)

and the devout back to Outremer (literally 'overseas', a term for the Latin East). As the 13th century dawned, 'enthusiasm for the crusade was at its height, certainly amongst the Catholic west's rulers and their nobility, and probably too in society at large' (Housley 2008: 569). For the Ayyubid princes and potentates whose realms surrounded the diminished Crusader States, the Franks were more a fact of life than an existential threat, so that 'solidarity in the face of the infidel was hardly even an ideal, and certainly not a reality' (Humphreys 1998: 7). With the passing of Salāh ad-Dīn their concerns stretched no further than their own domains, and how those domains could be enlarged at the expense of their relatives. Such a lack of concern would have consequences.

Egypt, and the powerful Ayyubid sultans that ruled her, would be the focus of political intrigue, raids, pitched battles and invasions, for the kings of the West and the Frankish princes of the East knew that to take and hold Jerusalem was impossible without first breaking the strength of their most potent foe. The first attempt on Egypt, the Fourth Crusade of 1204, collapsed into an embarrassment of greed and murder before it got anywhere near the Nile. The campaigns that would follow were to be marked by military success and disastrous failure alike. The invasion of Egypt in 1218 would achieve some success, but would squander all it gained through pride leavened with leaderless incompetence. Jerusalem would be won back, albeit briefly, by the diplomatic skill of the Holy Roman Emperor, Frederick II (r. 1220–50), in a bloodless appearance on the crusading stage, before terrible circumstance and the politics of the region would see it lost again. The vengeance that the Franks sought for this reverse would lead through a road of ashes to La Forbie, with the enormity of that defeat sparking a new fire in the West, as Hattin had done 57 years before. The crusade of Louis IX, King of France (r. 1226–70), struck through Damietta into Egypt and fought itself to a ruinous standstill at the gates of al-Mansūrah.

For the Franks the urge to defeat their enemy was clear enough, even though for the most part they understood little about the people they were fighting. The crusaders came into lands that were 'Saracen' to their eyes, but this blanket designation failed to convey

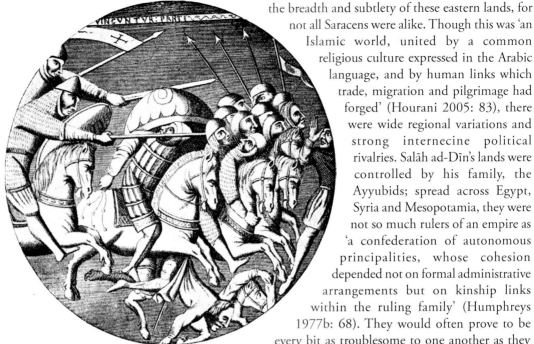

the breadth and subtlety of these eastern lands, for not all Saracens were alike. Though this was 'an Islamic world, united by a common religious culture expressed in the Arabic language, and by human links which trade, migration and pilgrimage had forged' (Hourani 2005: 83), there were wide regional variations and strong internecine political rivalries. Salāh ad-Dīn's lands were controlled by his family, the Ayyubids; spread across Egypt, Syria and Mesopotamia, they were not so much rulers of an empire as 'a confederation of autonomous principalities, whose cohesion depended not on formal administrative arrangements but on kinship links within the ruling family' (Humphreys 1977b: 68). They would often prove to be every bit as troublesome to one another as they were to the Franks. Such internecine conflict and the weaknesses that it bred had played an important part in the relative success that the Franks enjoyed against the Ayyubids' Fatimid predecessors, and it would grant the same opportunities to new generations of Frankish princes intent on rebuilding their harried principalities.

Crusaders chasing Seljuks, from a painted window at Saint-Denys, 12th century. The Franks had, for the most part, a poor understanding of the faith and culture of the men whom they were fighting, and the 'Saracens' in their turn had a fairly low view of the Franks, and the lands from which they came. The Franks were terrifyingly violent enemies to be sure, but their internal divisions and low numbers meant that by the 13th century they were a local rather than an existential threat, unlike the Mongol horde rising in the east. (Internet Archive Book Images)

The Templars, with their long service in the East, had a greater appreciation for this state of affairs than did those fresh to the Holy Land, and their position in any serious military or political endeavour of the time was assured. The erosion of Frankish power at the hands of Salāh ad-Dīn had weakened the military capabilities of the Crusader States; in concert with the other Military Orders, the Templars became the most consistent and effective defenders of the Latin East, and they were also at the forefront of each of the expeditions to destroy Egyptian power and reclaim Jerusalem. Their money, their political strength, their decades of campaigning experience, and their ability to field a substantial and potent military force, ensured their place in the vanguard of crusading armies.

The *mamlūk* (pl. *mamālīk*), trained since boyhood to become a master of his military arts, was the fighting man at the heart of the Ayyubid armies of Egypt. Though their numbers had increased in recent years, the *mamālīk* were still relatively few, but like their Templar enemies they were the first, best and most renowned of their kind. Their military strength was being matched by an increasingly potent political presence that would bode ill for the crusaders and Salāh ad-Dīn's heirs alike.

In the flooded Nile outside Damietta, on the bloody field of La Forbie and at the grim battle of al-Mansūrah, Templars and *mamālīk* would ride against one another as warriors for their opposing faiths; they were the finest exemplars of their respective armies and military cultures, a fact that would manifest itself time and again in the ferocity of their victories and the brutality of their defeats.

The Crusader and Ayyubid states, 1193–1250

The beginning of the 13th century seemed, at least on the surface, to be the start of a more settled period in the Latin East. The age of great victories that saw Salāh ad-Dīn win Jerusalem and decimate the lands of the Franks, cutting their kingdoms down to a series of crenellated rumps along the coast, was over. His legacy was the Ayyubid sultanate (after his family name, Ayyūb), a realm that stretched from Barqa on the north African coast through Egypt, down the west coast of Arabia to Yemen, up through Palestine and Syria to Aleppo on the border of Asia Minor, and across the Jazīra to the east, bordering on the lands of the Abbasids. Such a great expanse was broken into regions and ruled by members of Salāh ad-Dīn's family, a manageable situation when he was alive but one of increasing political complexity and competition after his death. Egypt was the richest and most powerful of the domains, closely followed by Damascus with the remaining domains of Aleppo, the Jazīra, Homs, Hama and Baalbek varying in size and importance over the Ayyubid period. For the Franks the reduction in their lands did not diminish their ambitions, and despite the losses they had suffered throughout the second half of the 12th century their possessions in Outremer were well defended and wealthy. In addition the kingdoms of the West, pricked by the loss of Jerusalem and the failure of Richard Coeur de Leon's crusade to regain it, were approaching the height of their enthusiasm for the crusading movement; enthusiasm that would see major expeditions launched throughout the period. Such initiatives, born in the West but delivered to fruition in the Latin East, had, with their enormous infusions of men, money and *matériel*, the capacity to reinvigorate the denuded fortunes of the Frankish princes. Against such a potent threat the Ayyubids, fractured by ambition and fuelled by mistrust and loathing for one another that often outstripped any animosity they had towards their Christian neighbours, were vulnerable. Egypt especially had come to dominate the thoughts of crusading princes, as it was the key to any sustained recovery of territory in Palestine, including Jerusalem, and so it was against the sultans of that land that the crusading armies would launch their attacks, battling repeatedly for a victory that, however close it seemed, always managed to elude them.

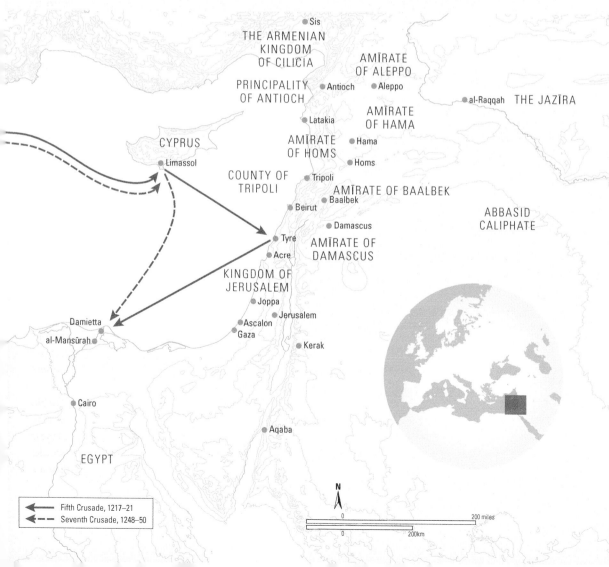

The Opposing Sides

ORIGINS, RECRUITMENT AND MOTIVATION

Templar

Unlike the *mamālik*, who had a long and varied history in the region, the Knights Templar were wholly a product of the crusades and the environment they created in the Latin East. Founded in 1118 or 1119 by a pair of French knights (Hugues de Payns and Godefroi de Saint-Omer) as a confraternity to defend Western pilgrims from banditry and persecution, the Templars' importance – and unique place in the crusading world – grew rapidly. First recognized by the Council of Nablus in 1120, the Order gained papal approval at the Council of Troyes in 1129, where in their new Rule (the document that laid out their duties and codes of conduct) they were designated as 'the Poor Knights of Christ of the Temple which is in Jerusalem' (Flori 2005: 22). To this foundation the Cistercian abbot Bernard de Clairvaux gave a spiritual and ethical context that in large part defined the nature of this new form of knighthood, saying that 'I am almost in doubt whether they ought to be called monks or knights; except that perhaps it would be more appropriate for me to call them both' (quoted in Flori 2005: 26).

The foundation and growth of the Templars was contemporaneous with the great flowering of knighthood that was taking place across Western Europe; the culture of that knighthood celebrated the great deeds of semi-mythic heroes like Roland and Charlemagne, encouraging knights in their pursuit of renown through magnificent feats of arms. Fame, with its accompanying recognition by one's peers, was the measure by which such men lived, and in this respect the Templars were radically different from the society that made them. They had the ascetic quality of monkhood and, more importantly, the humility that went with it. Their fundamental goal was to achieve victories for the glory of God, not themselves, so it is small wonder that the 'order regarded itself, and was regarded by others, as the defender of Christendom; if not the sole defender, then certainly the most important' (Muldoon 2005: 47–48).

The Order itself was made up of knights, sergeants and a range of other ancillary and supportive members, as well as temporary members who could join for a time (such as the English knight William Marshal, who served with the

Templars for a short period in the mid-1180s) but who were not proper members of the Order. In general those who joined did so as adults, fully trained in the arts of war and often with significant experience of campaigning life. The indications are that the knight brothers were literate but not well educated (i.e. they could read and write their native languages, but not many would have had a command of Latin, still less Greek), and that they were drawn from across Western Europe, funnelled from the network of commanderies that the Order had established through donations and legacies, with the probable majority coming from France. The resilience of such a system is shown by the ability of the Order to rebuild itself time and again after it suffered catastrophic reverses in the field; for example, the Order supplied a contingent of 300 knights for Louis IX's crusade of 1249, a scant six years after its field army had been annihilated at La Forbie.

Mamlūk

The 12th-century Persian writer Sharaf al-Zamān Tāhir Marvazī noted of the Turks: 'The Turcomans spread through the Islamic lands and there displayed an excellent character. So much so that they ruled over the greater part of these territories, becoming kings and sultans … Those who live in deserts and steppes and lead a nomadic life in winter and summer are the strongest of men and the most enduring in battle and warfare' (quoted in Hillenbrand 2007: 148). Such praise was warranted.

Though there had been a tradition of 'slave' soldiers in Islamic and pre-Islamic armies of the region, it was the 9th-century Abbasid Caliph al-Muʿtasim (r. 833–42) who started what would become a recognizable policy of buying young slaves from the steppe peoples and inculcating them with a basic knowledge of Islam, a fierce loyalty to their master and an expertise in military pursuits that acknowledged and expanded upon their core strengths as horsemen and archers of great skill. Over the following centuries *mamlūk* soldiers would become a common part of the Islamic armies of the Levant, though it was the military reforms to the Egyptian army undertaken by Salāh ad-Dīn that set the stage for their growth under his descendants.

Temple Mount from the south. The rapid growth of Templar establishments throughout Europe was testimony to the success of their new interpretation of chivalry, a secular institution that they made overtly religious in both form and function. Despite their papal blessing and the ideological ministrations of scholars like Bernard de Clairvaux, support for the new Order was not universal. Bernard's fellow Cistercian Isaac d'Étoile took a decidedly different view of these Poor Knights of Christ: 'There has sprung up a new monster, a certain new knighthood, whose Order – as a certain man says neatly – is from the fifth Gospel because it is set up to force unbelievers into the Christian faith by lances and cudgels, and may freely despoil those who are not Christians, and butcher them religiously; but if any of them fall in such ravaging, they are called martyrs of Christ' (quoted in Flori 2005: 36). Such views may have been in the minority, but they drew out the thorny issue of the Church's gradual evolution throughout this period from a primarily spiritual into an aggressively temporal power. (Metropolitan Museum of Art, www.metmuseum.org)

Recruited mainly from the Turkish Kipchaq and Oghuz tribal groups (increasingly Kipchaq after the pressures of the Mongol invasions began to be felt in the early 13th century), adolescent slaves would be sold off into the *mamlūk* military system at markets near *tabaqah* (barracks) in cities such as Cairo and Damascus. Once in the *tabaq* the young *mamlūk*, likely already a good rider and competent archer from his early years, would be trained in all aspects of cavalry warfare, hunting, polo and equine care. This training continued after the *mamlūk* left to join his household, usually at the *maydān* (hippodrome).

There were different types of *mamlūk*; the most important were those of the sultan, for whom by the time of as-Sālih Najm ad-Dīn Ayyūb (r. 1240–49; hereafter as-Sālih) there were two 'household' units: the Bahriyya (so named for the Bahrī fortress on the Nile that was their home, numbering around 800– 1,000), and the Jamdāriyya ('masters of the robe', the sultan's personal bodyguard, numbering around 200). They were the best trained, best equipped and most prestigious of the *mamālik*; they were his personal troops, an expression of his power, the instrument of his will. In addition, each senior *amīr* (officer; pl. *umarā*) or man important in the management of the state would have a personal retinue of *mamālik*, varying in both number and quality. The *iqtā* system (the practice of granting an individual a 'fief') provided each *amīr* with a living in return for his military service as well as his raising and management of a body of troops (the size of which was naturally dependent on the generosity of the *iqtā*).

By the Ayyubid period in Egypt most *mamālik* shared strong similarities in origin and training, and were part of a homogenous Turkish culture, including language (most could not speak Arabic) within the *mamlūk* establishments that helped to distinguish them from other troops and polities. In addition, their consistent and well-deserved reputation as skilled and brave warriors fostered a sense of distinct pride in their identity, an identity reinforced by the indulgence of their masters who had bought them, nurtured them, and lavished them with praise, opportunities and wealth.

The torture of a slave. The idea of *mamālik* as slaves in the Western sense is erroneous. Under Islamic precepts slavery was better understood as a system of 'patronage' which 'although not between equals, nevertheless imposed obligations on both parties … [whose] relationship was supposedly a sort of alliance. This ethical concept enabled slaves to have legal rights, almost as if they had been adopted as "foster sons" by a master who accepted legal obligations as their "foster father"' (Nicolle 2014: 5). William of Tyre noted that recruitment was from 'young prisoners-of-war, slaves bought in the slave-markets and the offspring of slave mothers' (quoted in Lev 1999: 155), though there were undoubtedly other sources. For a *mamlūk*, his purchase would lead to his conversion to Islam and an extended period of intensive military training in a *tabaq*, after which he would be manumitted and accepted into his master's household. That environment would be a place further to develop his skills, to make a living, and to allow him prospects for advancement that were at least the equal of those available to most of the free-born men of the time. A *mamlūk* took great pride in his status as a member of an acknowledged military elite, a pride that was intensified by the close cultural and linguistic ties that he shared with his fellow ethnic Turks. (© The British Library Board, Harley 4375 f. 70v)

MORALE AND LOGISTICS

Templar

The commentator al-Harawi, a man with wide and varied experience of the turmoil that raged through the Latin East in the 1180s and 1190s, and who subsequently wrote *Discussion on the Stratagems of War* for Salāh ad-Dīn, was of the firm opinion that a sultan 'should beware of [the Hospitaller and Templar] monks … for he cannot achieve his goals through them; for they have great fervour in religion, paying no attention to the [things of this] world' (quoted in Hamblin 1992: 237).

His observation was well made, and the treatment of captured Templars, who were more often than not executed at once rather than being offered for ransom (as was the usual custom), reinforces the point that their enemies knew them to be implacable.

Such reliability coupled with their campaigning experience meant that the Templars would usually act as the vanguard of a Frankish army, and would form on the right when in line of battle. On the march, especially in hostile territory, the knights and mounted sergeants would huddle together in tight formations, surrounded by walls of infantry and crossbowmen who would be able to fight off the harassment by the enemy's mounted archers, preventing them from taking too heavy a toll on the horses. Such formations relied on discipline and close cohesion between horse and foot, something that Frankish armies, always at war, learned and utilized effectively.

The Templar would have a riding horse (a palfrey) and a pack horse (a rouncey), together with one or two chargers (destriers, each accompanied by a squire to see to the horse's needs) that he would mount only at the point of battle. Clear rules were established as to how to behave on the march, including specific injunctions against breaking ranks, as well as how to organize and, in the event of a surprise attack, defend the army's camp. All the mundanities of campaign life were itemized and regulated with a strictness that must have been most unusual for a Frankish force at that time, and which give a good indication of how important a role hierarchy, discipline and obedience played in the everyday cohesion of a Templar force – a cohesion that would pay dividends on the battlefield.

Mamlūk

As professional troops, the *mamālīk* paid unusual attention to the mundanities of campaign life, such as making camp; choosing the right location was important because, as the 14th-century Egyptian writer al-Ansārī noted, 'the place in which the army alights must possess water and pasturage and firewood and other things upon which the [sustenance of the] army depends' (quoted in Scanlon 2012: 86). The camp should also be sited so at to allow the army to advance to battle or retreat from an attack as necessary, and it should have a rearguard set against natural defences (mountains, rivers) to help protect against surprise incursions, augmented by pickets further out. If an attack was likely the camp would be surrounded with a trench lined with stakes, with the

This Templar, like his brother-knights, is fighting as the retreating Crusader army's rearguard. Caught in the Nile floods, unable to press home their attack on al-Mansūrah and threatened by Ayyubid incursions down the Nile to their right and across their line of communications back to Damietta, the crusaders are beginning to lose cohesion as morale falters. The professionalism and constancy of the Military Orders, here as at other earlier points in the campaign, stops a retreat from becoming a rout. The knight is charging, with shield up and lance couched, driving back another of the incessant Ayyubid attacks that are tearing at the back and sides of the army. Both the knight and his horse are worn and dirty, having been fighting in muddy and flooded fields for several days, with no respite in sight.

Weapons, dress and equipment

The Templar wears the cappa (**1**), a relatively close-fitting white robe that would give way in the 1240s to the sleeveless surcoat, as well as a mantle. He is armed with a lance (**2**), at least 10–12ft long and ideally made from ash; an arming sword (**3**) around 37–38in long and weighing approximately 2.5lb; and also a 'grete sword of war' (**4**), a larger weapon around 46in in length and weighing approximately 3.25lb that could be used with one or two hands, that was slung from his saddle.

He wears a full suit of mail (**5**) comprised of a thigh-length hauberk with an integral coif as well as full sleeves and mufflers (mail mittens) that weighs 25–30lb, worn over a gambeson (padded jacket), together with mail chausses that cover his legs and feet and weigh 13lb. His helmet (**6**), worn over the coif and possibly also a metal arming cap, is an evolution of the 'enclosed' helmets popular at the turn of the century (and which will evolve into the nascent flat-topped version of the 'great helm' that will begin to appear from around 1240 onwards), and weighs 2–3lb. He carries a 'heater'-type shield (**7**) made from wood with a painted leather cover and weighing 8lb, with a neck-strap that allows the shield to be slung over his shoulder or across his back when not in immediate use.

The Templar's destrier wears a caparison (**8**) without padding or barding and bears with a saddle that has a high cantle (**9**) notable for its enclosed arms designed to keep the rider in his seat, especially during the shock of giving or receiving a charge. The full weight of the Templar's weapons and equipment is around 53–60lb.

The lion passant was the heraldic blazon of Sultan Baybars I, the founder of the Mamluk state. *Jihād* had personal, societal and political dimensions, for leaders and followers both; it encompassed not just the idea of righteous struggle with non-believers, but also of the moral struggle within oneself, and one's religious duty within personal and communal life. The traditional idea that *jihād* could be called and led only by legitimate leadership was also changing – or rather being changed by men like Baybars, who, with no familial right to power, used their successful implementation of *jihād* to bolster their claims to the throne and legitimize their authority in scholarly and public eyes alike. (Werner Forman Archive / Bridgeman Images)

entrances guarded by cavalry and archers. In addition, a body of cavalry would be hidden outside the camp perimeter in order to launch surprise attacks on the flanks or rear of any enemy force that tried to press home an assault.

The unglamorous role of protecting supplies was also taken seriously; for the guarding of baggage the first requisite was to have a good man at the head of a force of cavalry to protect the army's treasury, backed up by trustworthy and experienced troops. This was no idle posting, for as al-Ansārī noted, 'the baggage must be encompassed by those who fear the stain of running away more than they fear death, for there is no sustenance possible for the army without its baggage' (quoted in Scanlon 2012: 102).

TRAINING, DOCTRINE AND TACTICS

Templar

The views of an anonymous pilgrim from the 1160s–1180s (written down in *Tractatus de locis et statu sanctae terrae*, or 'Tract on the places and state of the Holy Land') gives a potent view of the military duty of the Templars:

> The Templars are excellent knights, wearing white mantles with a red cross. Their bicoloured standard which is called the bauçant goes before them into battle. They go into battle in order and without making a noise, they are the first to desire engagement and more vigorous than others; they are the first to go and the last to return, and they wait for their master's command before acting. When they make the decision that it would be profitable to fight and the trumpet sounds to give the order to advance, they piously sing the psalm of David: 'Not to us, Lord, not to us but to your name give the glory', couch their lances and charge into the enemy. As one person, they strongly seek out the units and wings of the battle, they never dare to give way, they either completely break up the enemy or they die. In returning from battle they are the last and they go behind the rest of the crowd, looking after all the rest and protecting them. (Quoted in Nicholson 2004: 67–68)

Knights and sergeants came into the Order as trained men. The whole ethos of medieval Western society was martial, dominated by wars great and small, public and private, and in such a society knights began their training early, learning to ride, hunt and fight in their early to mid-teens; it was acknowledged at the time that the rigours of such a process were vital, as noted by the 12th-century English chronicler Roger of Hoveden, a veteran of the Third Crusade: 'A youth must have seen his blood flow and felt his teeth crack under the blow of his adversary and have [been] thrown to the ground twenty times. Thus will he be able to face real war with the hope of victory' (quoted in Oakeshott 2000: 102). As with their *mamlūk* enemies, young knights would learn a great deal about riding and group cooperation from hunting, as well as from the tournaments that were popular at the time: large and often startlingly violent war games where the object was to batter one's opponents into submission and ransom them and their goods in reward.

A knight of the Order would be an experienced horseman who was proficient in swordsmanship (both his arming sword and the 'grete war sword'), as well as the use of the lance, mace, bow and crossbow, both from the saddle and on foot. There is almost no record of any training regimes or practices in the Rule of the Templars, which is probably more a sign that so much of it was taken for granted rather than that it did not happen; such men

Illustration of a knight, mid-13th century. This splendid image of an English knight by William Peraldius in his work *Summa de vitiis* gives a good contemporary view of how such a man would be armed and mounted. He wears a well-developed enclosed helm (an advance on the more-or-less open-faced nasal helms that predominated in the previous century, and a precursor of the great helm which would start to appear from *c*.1240) and carries his sword and lance in a manner more for display than use, one suspects. The shield is of the 'heater' type (the term 'heater' deriving from the Victorian period, bizarrely enough, when the shape of the shield was similar to that of the domestic clothes-iron); his mail includes chausses, mufflers and a coif, covered by a surcoat. His mount is notable for the saddle's high, curved cantle, the 'arms' of which lock the knight in place allowing him to deliver (and receive) a charge without being easily dismounted, and the girth is double-banded to ensure that the saddle as a whole is fixed securely to the horse. (© The British Library Board, Harley 3244 f. 28)

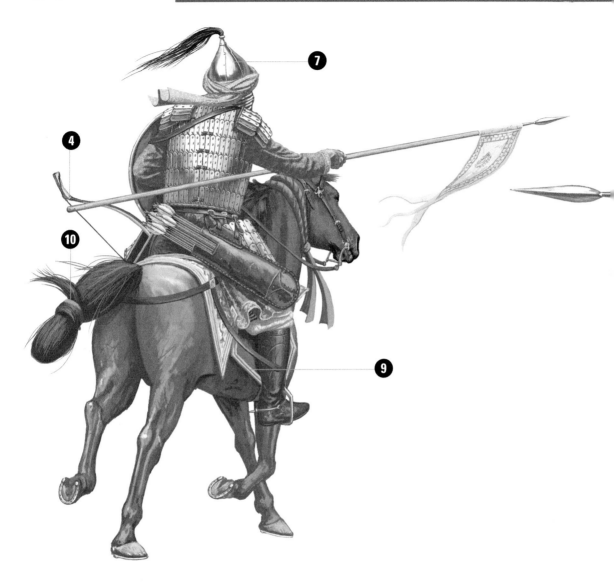

Weapons, dress and equipment

This warrior wears a richly patterned blue and gold 'Turkish' coat (*al-aqbiya al-turkiyya;* **1**), the hem of which crossed the chest in a diagonal from right to left and which was popular with both the Ayyubids and Seljuqs. His boots are worked red leather and his lance pennant is patterned silk in yellow, the traditional colour of the Ayyubids. He is armed with a 12ft-long lance (*rumh;* **2**) weighing 3–4lb; a straight-bladed sword (*sayf;* **3**), 40in long and weighing 1.5–2lb; and a composite bow (*qaws* or *hanīyah;* **4**) and quiver (*kinanāh*) weighing a little over 3lb.

Beneath his Turkish coat he wears a hauberk (*dir;* **5**) weighing 25–30lb, while over his coat he wears a lamellar cuirass

(*jawshan;* **6**) with shoulder and thigh tassets weighing 16–20lb. His helmet (*baydah;* **7**) is steel with a horsehair plume, and is worn over a coif (*mighfar*) for a combined weight of approximately 6–8lb. He carries a large round shield (*turs;* **8**) 25.6in in diameter and weighing 6–8lb.

The *mamlūk's* saddle is of leather with a quilted seat and embroidered cloth panels (**9**), while his horse wears a twisted scarf of blue silk, has a highly patterned saddlecloth and has its tail tied with a blue silk ribbon (**10**) in a traditionally Turkish touch. The full weight of the *mamlūk's* weapons and equipment is around 59–74lb.

This *mamlūk*, a junior *amīr* from Sultan al-Kāmil's personal *'askar*, rides in one of the countless small attacks that were harassing the flanks and rear of the lumbering, waterlogged Crusader army. An expert with his composite bow, the *mamlūk* would harry the crusaders with long-range archery to threaten and provoke individual Christian knights into rash reactions or counter-charges in which their distance from their own ranks would make them decidedly more vulnerable. When closing for close combat he would make the most of his excellent mount and much-practised equestrian skills to try to outride and then outfight his opponent, using both lance and sword.

understood that their *raison d'être* was to fight, and as such they must have practised individual skills as well as group tactics, especially the charge, which required discipline and experience to master.

Knights were the key component in a Templar force, but not the only one. Sergeants, more lightly armed and armoured than the knights, played a significant role, both mounted and on foot, and were supplemented by the Turcopoles: lightly armed and armoured horsemen drawn from the indigenous Christian population whose key roles were probably as horse archers and scouts. In addition, there were numbers of foot troops (mostly ignored in the sources) that were presumably a mix of 'Syrians' (native Christians) and mercenary crossbowmen.

The best-known (and when it worked, most effective) tactic of the knights of the Order was the cavalry charge. Riders would be formed into a series of *echelles* (squadrons), making up a cavalry line led by the Marshal that was supported by a second line comprised of the mounted sergeants. The objective of the charge was to shatter the enemy formation, ideally by breaking straight through it, and then to set upon the enemy in a mêlée, with supporting lines of cavalry exploiting the confusion (or providing cover for retreat after a failed attack). A successful charge could have a devastating effect, such as that executed by the Templars at the battle of Montgisard in 1177. Ralph de Diceto, Dean of London, noted how Eudes de Saint-Amand (Grand Master 1171–79) at the head of 84 knights of his 'personal company' launched a decisive attack on the Saracens: 'Spurring all together, as one man, they made a charge, turning neither to the left nor to the right. Recognising the battalion in which Saladin commanded many knights, they manfully approached it, immediately penetrated it, incessantly knocked down, scattered, struck and crushed ... [the enemy was] dispersed everywhere, everywhere turned in flight, everywhere given to the mouth of the sword' (quoted in Nicholson 2004: 66).

ABOVE An idealized battle scene between Crusaders and Saracens. There was no Templar or crusader equivalent to the *furūsiyya* literature of the *mamālik*; *La règle du Temple* ('The Rule of the Templars') suggests conduct in certain military situations, but it is a general set of instructions for the Templar to follow in all aspects of his life, not a specific manual of war. (Metropolitan Museum of Art, www.metmuseum.org)

BELOW The entire Frankish force would be screened by foot soldiers, archers and crossbowmen (**A**) to ensure that the Turkish horse archers were kept more or less at bay thus preserving the integrity of the cavalry. The knights and mounted sergeants (**B**) would sally forth through the gaps left in the foot soldiers' ranks as opportunity or necessity warranted. The Templars traditionally anchored the right of the line, and would usually form the army's vanguard when on the march. The baggage (**C**) would remain safely in the centre of the force for the duration of the encounter. (After David Nicolle)

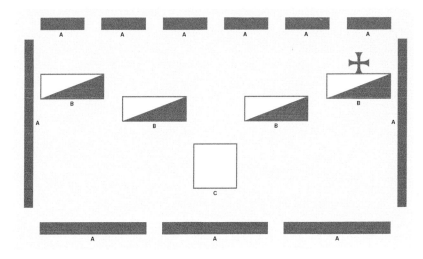

The impact of such a potent tactic was not ignored by the Muslim armies of the time, whose main defence was to refuse to act as a target for the Western knights, instead withdrawing out of range and harassing them with arrows and feint attacks.

> That these methods were not just coincidentally employed is confirmed by the Franciscan friar Fidenzio of Padua, who described the Muslim technique when faced by a Frankish charge: 'The Saracens retreat and scatter; they rush, some here, others there. Afterwards, at the sound of a trumpet ... they are reunited and they attack the Christians, striking the men and their horses with many arrows and killing them.' (Marshall 1994: 160)

Mamlūk

'What man, however experienced and learned, could dare to write of the skill, prowess and courage of the Turks' (quoted in France 2005: 63). That observation, from the *Gesta Francorum*, aims in part to excite a sense of the might of the crusaders by attributing great worth to their enemies. Even so, it contains within it the truth that the Franks knew and appreciated the quality of the men they were fighting. Such acclaim also existed in the Arabic armies where 'the Turkic peoples of Inner Asia had for centuries been admired within Islam as warriors of the highest degree of valor and military skill' (Humphreys 1977b: 96).

The core of *mamlūk* training was *furūsiyya*, literally 'horsemanship', which comprised a series of exercises for the horseman that would train him in the mounted use of the lance, the sword and the bow, as well as care for his horse, hunting and polo (both of which were extremely important in developing a horseman's ability to work within a group, not to mention honing his riding skills). The definition of *furūsiyya* by Ibn Taġrībirdī, a 15th-century *mamlūk* writer, could be applied equally to his 13th-century antecedents:

> *furūsiyya* is something different from bravery and intrepidity (*al-s hadjā'a wa'l-ikdām*), for the brave man overthrows his adversary by sheer courage, while the

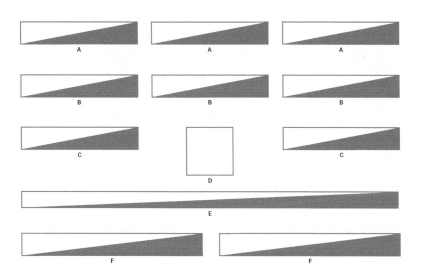

Ayyubid armies, especially those detached for a specific purpose such as the force sent to Gaza by Sultan as-Sālih in 1244, would be almost entirely cavalry forces. They would ideally organize themselves into five lines: a vanguard (**A**) made up of the hardiest and best-armed cavalrymen in the army; a second line (**B**) much the same; a third line (**C**) designated to protect the baggage (**D**); a fourth line (**E**) made up of light cavalry to provide rear security for the baggage; and a final, fifth line (**F**) as the army's rearguard. The care taken to protect the baggage (the third line was supposed always to be made up of good troops commanded by fine officers) was considerable.

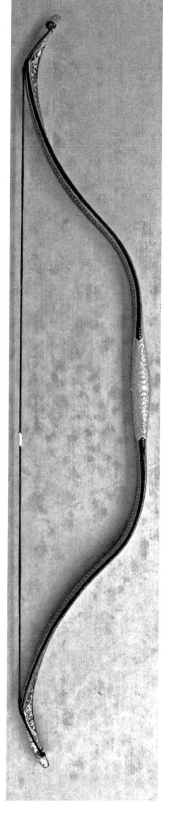

Reproduction of a Turkish bow. The Turkish *mamlūk* was skilled in the use of a number of different ranged weapons both in hunting and war, including crossbows and 'pellet' bows, but it was the composite bow used from horseback that defined him, to his enemies as much as to himself. Such bows (composites of horn, sinew and wood) were magnificent examples of functional design, often taking over a year and a half to make due to the drying process. In the hands of a competent archer such bows, with a probable draw weight of 80–100lb, became fearsomely effective weapons, with significant penetrative power at close ranges, as well as the capacity to wound men and especially horses at ranges of well over 300yd. Their compact nature, coupled with their high draw weights, made them ideal for horse archery, though the mastery of such skills was often a lifelong pursuit. The men who used these bows were able to release multiple arrows at different targets in quick succession – and hit them – all while their horse was at a full gallop. They were dangerous to chase, too, as many of them used the 'Parthian shot', an ancient technique whereby the fleeing rider turns suddenly in his saddle and lets fly a shaft at his pursuer. (Lukas Novotny, The Saluki Bow Co.)

horseman (*fāris al-khayl*) is one who handles his horse well in the charge (*karr*) and the retreat (*farr*), and who knows all that he needs to know about his horse and his weapons and about how to handle them in accordance with the rules known and established among the masters of this art. (Quoted in Jensen 2013: 9)

Though some aspects of *furūsiyya* could lend themselves to being seen as the foundation of a knightly code similar to that which was flourishing in the West, it seems that for the *mamālik* of the period *furūsiyya* was above all a practical art, not a 'chivalrous' one. *Furūsiyya* exercises were conducted in the *maydān*, where horsemen would practise individual skills as well as coordinated tactics within larger groups. Particular attention was paid to archery, and *mamālik* excelled in its practice: being able to shoot with either hand was a common skill, and by standing in his stirrups (which were shorter that those of European knights) a *mamlūk* could shoot his bow with impressive accuracy despite riding at a full gallop, his legs absorbing the movement of the horse and thus allowing his upper body to remain steady. This method also meant that the draw weights of *mamlūk* bows could be higher, as the rider's archery technique wasn't compromised by trying to stay in his saddle. Horsemen could loose several arrows in very quick succession and also change weapons mid-gallop – for example, sheathing a sword and drawing a bow or vice versa – allowing them to react to opportunities or threats with great speed. The reins could be dropped when loosing arrows or changing weapons, because the horse was well trained and would continue on its course without correction from the rider.

The *mamālik* were also well versed in the charge, having several techniques to choose from depending on the situation and the type of enemy they were facing, as well as a keen understanding of the dangers of getting carried away, as noted by al-Ansārī: 'It is required of the warrior [charging] against the enemy that he does not exhaust himself in rushing his horse and that he does not pursue his adversary beyond a third of the distance between him and the enemy…To go beyond this is heedlessness' (quoted in Scanlon 2012: 105). Swordsmanship was also embraced, with the sword itself celebrated for its beauty and almost mystical properties, as mentioned in the *mamlūk* military treatise *Munyatu 'l-Guzāt*: 'Know that there is no weapon among weapons that is described with (such) nobility, and that is so valuable that its possessor is proud of it and achieves victory with it, except the sword, because it has respect and superiority over all the weapons' (Öztopçu 1986: 183). Training with the sword included learning how to draw and sheathe the weapon properly, how to draw and strike in a single movement, how to deliver a series of accurate blows to both left and right while riding, and (through playing polo) how to swing one's blade without hitting one's mount.

Such a panoply of skills meant that *mamālīk* were versatile and had great potential on the battlefield. Tactically, Ayyubid armies would usually choose a 'line' formation or one with the flanks curving inwards like a pair of horns. Ideally the army would have the sun and wind at its back and be divided into a centre and two flanks, in turn organized into five lines – the first line was the vanguard (spread across the centre and both flanks), succeeded by the second line in the same disposition, with the third line detailed to protect the baggage; the fourth line, made up of light horsemen, protected the rear of the baggage, while the fifth line was the rearguard. The commentator al-Ansārī noted that 'It is necessary that the cavalrymen in [the vanguard] be outstanding for strength and courage and conquering spirit and experience in war, for they will be at the throat of the enemy, and those behind them of the [other] lines depend on them' (quoted in Scanlon 2012: 100).

Tactics would of course depend upon the nature of the battle, but *mamālīk* (and Turkic troops in general) became well known and much feared for wearing down their opponents with volleys of arrows, closing for close combat only when advantage offered, and refusing to receive Frankish charges. Their feigned retreat, though well known to the crusaders, was still an effective and dangerous technique that often drew blood in large part because the training, discipline and group skills needed to execute such a manoeuvre had been honed over many hours in the *maydān*.

Horse archers represented on a bottle, Egypt, 13th century. The difficulties of using a bow from horseback were considerable. Before even drawing an arrow the *mamlūk* had to be an expert rider and his mount had to be highly trained and responsive; then 'in action the archer had four movements to synchronise: kicking the horse into its charge, nocking the arrow, drawing the bow, and transferring the rein from the left to right hand' (Hyland 1996: 119). According to Taybughā in his mid-14th-century treatise on the subject *Kitāb al-Ramy wa-al-Rukūb*, every aspect – from how to nock an arrow to drawing the bowstring and releasing one's shot – was thought through and practised rigorously. He outlined ten primary and seven secondary types of shots, broadly broken down into three types: shooting upwards (called gourd shooting after the *furūsiyya* practice of loosing arrows at a gourd fixed atop a tall staff), downwards at the slant, and to either side. (Metropolitan Museum of Art, www. metmuseum.org)

LEADERSHIP AND COMMUNICATIONS

Templar

By most accounts the leadership that the Templars displayed was thoughtful and considered – excepting the occasional famed villain such as the notorious Gérard de Ridefort (Grand Master 1184–89). There are references to their caution in contrast to the heated impetuousness of crusaders from the West, and of their wise counsel to the leaders of armies in matters both military and diplomatic. They undoubtedly benefited from being permanently headquartered in the Latin East, and despite their iconoclastic enmity with Islam they had a more subtle and nuanced appreciation of their foes than did many others.

The command of the Order in the field was the responsibility of the Grand Master, if he were present, but in his absence authority fell on the shoulders of the Marshal, the Order's senior military figure, who would also lead the main attack in battle. The Turcopolier had command over Turcopole cavalry as well as the sergeant-brothers, and was probably also responsible for scouting duties when on the march. Knights would be grouped into *echelles*, which were led by a nominated knight with an accompanying standard-bearer and a personal guard of knights. The Gonfanier rode with the Order's banner on the march, but his more mundane (though no less important) duty was to look after the squires, both on campaign and in battle.

The role of banners was critically important in the hurly-burly of battle. The black-and-white standard of the Order, the *gonfanon bauçant* (literally 'piebald banner'), would be at the head of the line of march, and was carried by the Marshal in war. According to *La Règle du Temple* ('The Rule of the Templars') the Marshal would have a banner-guard of up to ten knights, one of whom would always be at his side carrying a furled spare

German crossbow, *c.*1460. The crossbow was widely used by both the Franks and their *mamlūk* enemies, including on occasion from horseback. The Byzantine princess Anna Comnena described it well: 'this instrument of war, which shoots missiles to an enormous distance, has to be stretched by lying almost on one's back; each foot is pressed forcibly against the half-circles of the bow and the two hands tug at the bow, pulling it with all one's strength towards the body … arrows of all kinds are shot. They are very short, but extremely thick with a heavy iron tip. In the shooting the string exerts tremendous violence and force, so that the missiles wherever they strike do not rebound; in fact they transfix a shield, cut through a heavy iron breastplate and resume their flight on the far side, so irresistible and violent is the discharge. An arrow of this type has been known to make its way right through a bronze statue, and when shot at the wall of a very great town its point either protruded from the inner side or buried itself in the wall and disappeared altogether. Such is the crossbow, a truly diabolical machine' (quoted in DeVries & Smith 2007: 134–35). (Metropolitan Museum of Art, www.metmuseum.org)

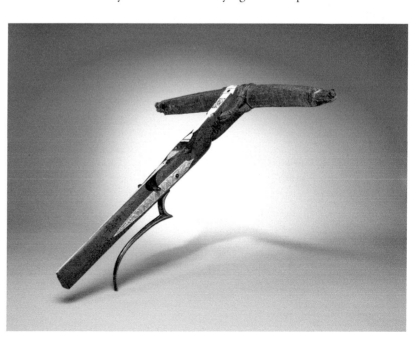

so that if the Marshal's banner falls or is torn or any misadventure befalls it, which God forbid, he can unfurl his banner … and if the Marshal is so badly wounded or afflicted that he cannot lead the attack, the one who carries the furled banner should lead the attack. And those who are ordered to guard the banner should go to him; neither the Marshal nor the one who carries the furled banner into battle should charge with it or lower it to charge for any reason. (Quoted in Upton-Ward 2002: 60)

The last point reinforces the need for Templars to have symbols that could not only inspire them but act as rallying-points in the confusion of a cavalry mêlée. In the event that a knight was separated from his *echelle* he was supposed to seek out the Marshal's banner, or failing that any Templar banner or banner of another Military Order.

Mamlūk

The sultan had personal authority over his forces, and would appoint a senior commander or vizier to act in his stead when he was incapacitated or needed elsewhere; for example, Fakhr ad-Din Yusuf's command of the advance forces at Damietta in 1249. A senior *amīr* of the army would sometimes also hold important court offices, reflecting their personal closeness to the sultan and the corresponding influence they could wield. As Ayyubid armies were informal affairs brought together when needed, they lacked a formal organizational structure, as well as the stratified system of ranks that would accompany such a structure. An *amīr* gained commands due to his experience, military prowess and political influence, and would usually be accompanied by his own personal retinue of *mamālik*. Once the army was gathered together,

A man riding a dromedary, mid-13th century. Communications were well developed within the Ayyubid Egyptian kingdom, with a range of options that could be employed as the situation warranted. The quickest, if least informative, method was the warning of enemy movements by the setting of relay fires at night (or smoke signals in the day) on points of high ground in line of sight; a system that, for example, could alert Cairo to events occurring in Damascus (20 days' march away) almost immediately. Messenger pigeons, which could cover that same distance in a single day, would be used to give a slightly more detailed report, while the most comprehensive briefings, taking three days to arrive, would be delivered by the swift camels of the postal relay service (*al-barīd*), a system that the Ayyubids inherited from the Fatimids. Such a consistently reliable system provided great political benefits as well as highly useful strategic and tactical information on the movements and intentions of the sultan's enemies. (© The British Library Board, Harley 3244 f. 48)

dispositions would be made according to the nature of the expected campaign, as well as the troops and *umarā'* that were available. As for the commander of the army, al-Ansārī viewed his responsibilities thus:

> … the general of the army must be perfect of intelligence, strong of heart, full of courage, greatly vigilant, very cautious, strong in resolution; perceptive about the rules of wars and the occurrence of opportunities in them, aware of stratagems and deceptions and tricks [practised] in them; informed about the management of armies and the organisation of troops … painstaking about the maintenance of morale among his soldiers; disinclined to give battle through favoring stratagems whenever possible … patient about the [possible] lengthening of battle and of siege; capable about retreat after the accomplishment of purpose [of the campaign].
> (Quoted in Scanlon 2012: 70–71)

In battle the commander would aim to position himself on high ground ideally in the centre of the line to allow him a clear field of view of all his forces. Bodies of troops were identified by banners, with communication by trumpet call – each *'askar* would have a standard-bearer and a trumpeter, as would each *tulb* (cavalry squadron). The noise and confusion of battle reduced signals to a series of basic commands; for the troops of the army, and especially the *mamālīk* with their extensive training in the *mayādīn* (hippodromes), calls to charge, retreat, feign a retreat, pursue a retreating enemy, and regroup were all practised time and again so reaction to them would become second nature.

ROLE WITHIN THE ARMY

Templar

Frankish armies of the period were similar in many respects to those of Western Europe, though there were some important differences. As with their Western counterparts, the Franks of the Crusader States found that assembling an army could be a haphazard and lengthy process, relying in large part upon bonds of fealty between lords and their subjects. Nevertheless, when a force of crusaders arrived in the East the shared military and cultural framework enabled composite armies to form that could fight effectively. The core of a crusading army would be made up from the Western knights who had taken the cross in conjunction with those native knights of the Crusader States in

Knights jousting. From an early 14th-century French manuscript, the image depicts a scene from a tournament (as shown by the blunted lances), which were at this time becoming – slowly – more genteel affairs than their violently unpredictable forebears. Even as the tournament became a more socially acceptable pastime it remained a significant factor in the training of knights, who could gain reputations as well as valuable experience from partaking. Tournaments offered their participants a chance to exercise their skills with the lance and sword, and just as importantly a chance to ride as part of a team of knights in excursions that had close parallels to actual combat. In a society where 'anyone who aspired to be gentle or noble had to have a military capacity, even if they chose not to exercise it' (France 1999: 62), the daily practice of arms was as essential as it was unremarkable. (© The British Library Board, Royal 14 E III f. 89)

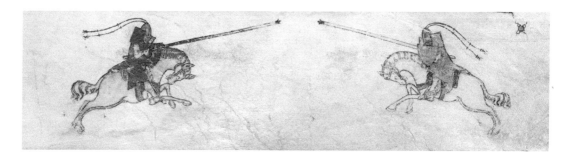

concert with the Military Orders. In addition to the knights there would be mounted sergeants, Turcopole light cavalry (who could act as mounted archers), sergeants, crossbowmen and foot soldiers. A certain proportion of the force would be mercenaries – the ranks of the crossbowmen were usually well seasoned with such men – though the distinction between men hired for a campaign and those owing service who had to be paid if they were to be able (or willing) to take their place in their lord's host was not always clear-cut.

There were never very many settlers in the Crusader States – one authority (France 2005: 58–80) estimates the number to be fewer than 250,000 or so – and such a small polity could not sustain large or permanent forces, instead relying to an ever-greater degree on the Military Orders for the maintenance and defence of strongholds, as well as in the field. One advantage the Crusader States did have, in contrast to their brethren in the West, was experience of campaigning that never seemed to end, for the 'settlers were constantly at war and so gained experience in fighting together. As a result the armies of the crusader states were more disciplined and coherent than those of the West' (France 2005: 73). Such discipline and coherence was exemplified by the Templars (and Hospitallers), whose approach to warfare was professional in the modern sense, subsuming individual skill within a framework of collaborative endeavour that was quite unusual for the time.

Individual endeavour, personal glory and fame were the hallmarks of the Western medieval military elite. Warfare in general and combat in particular was often a discrete affair that could sit at odds with the effective management of an army: '… the ethos of [the Western style of] war was overwhelmingly individual because personal prowess counted for more than tactical ability or logistic skill in small-scale encounters, and pride of birth was resistant to discipline' (France 2005: 69). Those 'small-scale encounters' were the norm in the West and Latin East alike, where warfare was 'above all made up of pillaging, often of sieges, sometimes of battles' (Contamine 1984: 219). Such low-intensity conflict, 'where each combatant or group of combatants, often in an incoherent and discontinuous fashion, fought primarily for immediate material profit' (Contamine 1984: 219), was dominated by *chevauchées* (large raids) and the *guerre guerroyante* (literally 'belligerent war'), a contemporary term that described the constant attrition of small-scale warfare 'made up of losses and recaptures, surprises, incursions, ambushes and sallies' (Contamine 1984: 219). It is within such a murderously personal environment that the difficulties associated with the management and behaviour of large forces need to be understood.

The Sign of the Templars. Captured here by Matthew Paris, the image is and always was symbolic, with strict provisions in the *Rule of the Templars* against two knights sharing a horse except in the most dire of circumstances. Though the heart of the Order, the knights did not march or fight alone. Sergeants could and did perform a role almost indistinguishable from that of the knights of the Order, though they were sometimes more lightly armed and armoured; for example, mention is made of the fact that their mail leggings stopped at the ankle to allow them to act on foot if need be. Turcopoles, essentially light cavalry, were presumably equipped even more lightly still, and there is no indication that – unlike the knights and sergeants – they were armed or armoured by the Order, instead supplying their own equipment. Foot soldiers, almost never mentioned, were certainly used, especially crossbowmen to help keep the *mamlūk* cavalry out of bowshot. (© The British Library Board, Royal 14 C VII f. 42v)

Mamlūk

The number of *mamālik* in Ayyubid armies was never very large, rarely exceeding a few thousand; even in Sultan as-Sālih's time, when the number of *mamālik* increased very quickly, they were never more than a minority (between 10 and 20 per cent) of the sultan's forces. The army of Egypt that confronted the crusaders of the 13th century had its roots in Salāh ad-Dīn's military reforms of the 1170s, and was made up of Turks, Kurds, Arabs (Bedouin and to a lesser extent Berbers), Armenians and black Africans (Nubians and Sudanese), among others. In the wake of Salāh ad-Dīn's death the Egyptian Ayyubid army became even more cavalry-focused, with estimates that 10,000–12,000 regular cavalry were kept under arms in Egypt, including around 1,000 household troops that would almost certainly have been *mamālik*. The army would be a composite force drawn together to meet a specific need, made up of the sultan's personal troops (*mamālik* and the *halqa*), the *mamālik* of his princes and *umarā'*, regional troops, mercenaries and auxiliaries.

The sultan's personal *mamālik*, in addition to the *mamālik* of his *umarā'* and princes, formed the core of the army in the form of its strongest and best-equipped cavalry force. An *'askar* was 'the contingent of troops recruited and maintained by each prince or important *amīr*' (Humphreys 1977b: 77), though the term isn't entirely straightforward; in most cases it refers to a body of troops drawn from and maintained by a particular region, but it was also

Mamālik from the Baptistère de Saint-Louis. The enemies of Christendom were well used to war and had developed consistent tactics in its employment. In the approach to battle, al-Ansārī notes, if the commander 'is not far distant from his enemy, he should not march except in [the condition of having] a vanguard, *muqaddamah*, a right flank, *maysarah*, and a left flank, *maymanah*, and a rearguard, *sāqah*; all with unsheathed weapons, their standards and banners unfurled, so that each one of them can be sure about his station and position within the army' (quoted in Scanlon 2012: 89–90). The centre should be strong, with the army making the most of the local terrain, with good officers detailed to reinforce weak or problematic areas. If the opposing force is small, the ideal was to overwhelm them with a massed cavalry attack, but when facing a stronger enemy al-Ansārī says to procrastinate using 'stratagems and tricks and deception wherever possible' (quoted in Scanlon 2012: 78), noting that 'one does not seek victory by engaging [the enemy] so long as victory can be attained through stratagems' (quoted in Scanlon 2012: 79). In victory a portion of the army should pursue a routed enemy, while the rest should plunder the field. (Pictures From History / Bridgeman Images)

used to describe a campaigning force drawn from said region, or sometimes the personal military retinue of an *amīr*. The size and composition of such an *ʿaskar* would depend upon the wealth of the region from which it was drawn, as well as the power of the prince or *amīr* who commanded it.

The *halqa* (a standing body of cavalry at least several thousand strong) was, after the *mamālīk* of the sultan and the *umarāʾ*, the main professional military force in the Ayyubid armies. The *halqa* held an important position under Salāh ad-Dīn, for whom it was a small *corps d'élite* – possibly even Salāh ad-Dīn's own regiment (Humphreys 1977b: 82–83) – under his personal control; and though it seems to have lost a degree of prestige after his death, it grew in size and utility. It was made up of freeborn men (Turks, Kurds, the sons of *mamālīk*) and was under the direct authority of the sultan, but unlike the *mamālīk* it was not quartered or equipped at his expense.

Additional cavalry was supplied in the shape of Turkmen and Kurdish tribesmen, presumably in the role of light cavalry and horse archers. The gradual impact of the Mongol incursions led to greater numbers of freeborn tribesmen available for service in Islamic armies, though there seems to have been a growing preponderance of Turkmen over Kurds. The observation that 'late in the Ayyubid period … standards of horse archery were clearly improved and given greater importance, being used both for harassment and in close-combat shock tactics' (Nicolle 1999b: 121) can be seen as an indication of the increasing influence of the Turkish approach to warfare within the army. Arab auxiliaries, almost exclusively Bedouin under the Egyptian Ayyubids, were used for raiding, harassment and guerrilla actions against enemy communications, according to R.S. Humphreys in his 1977 paper 'The Emergence of the Mamluk Army'. They were lightly armed (sometimes only with bamboo-shaft spears) and usually went without armour of any kind, excepting shields. Such troops were used extensively against the invading Crusader armies in the campaigns of 1218 and 1249, during which they caused considerable nuisance to the Franks both in camp and on the march.

Shirt of mail and plate, Persian, *c.*15th century. Though originating from a later period, this coat of mail is reasonably close to that which would have been worn by *mamālīk* of the Ayyubid dynasty (excepting the plates, which would have been relatively uncommon at this time). Called a *dir*, the hauberk would often be complemented with a *mighfar* (coif) and could be worn on its own or under a lamellar cuirass known as a *jawshan*: such armour had lames made of leather or more usually iron. (Metropolitan Museum of Art, www.metmuseum.org)

Damietta

1218–21

BACKGROUND TO BATTLE

Pope Innocent III (1160–1216), who formally instigated the Fifth Crusade at the Fourth Lateran Council, setting in motion the process that would gather groups of men from across the West and set them on course for a new war in Outremer. (Effigy by Joseph Kiselewski, Library of Congress)

The Fifth Crusade was driven by one man, Pope Innocent III, who had seen at first hand the ruination of the Fourth Crusade through fractious leadership, poor recruitment and parlous finances. Though he was undoubtedly the prime force behind the great endeavour, Innocent III would never see it come to pass, dying in July 1216; his demise at such a crucial time certainly had an impact, for it seems likely that he had planned to select both a leader and objective for the army when it rendezvoused at Messina and Brindisi in 1217. Denied much-needed focus at such an important stage, the gathering forces, which were already subject to a host of logistical and organizational problems, found themselves moving forward with only a general sense of where they were going and why. According to the chronicler Oliver von Paderborn:

In the year of grace 1218, in the month of March, ships began to sail to the port of Acre from the province of Cologne with other small ships from the province of Bremen and Trier. Thus was accomplished the plan formed in the Lateran Council at Rome under the Lord Pope Innocent of good memory, for leading the army of the Christians into the land of Egypt. (Quoted in Peters 1971: 61)

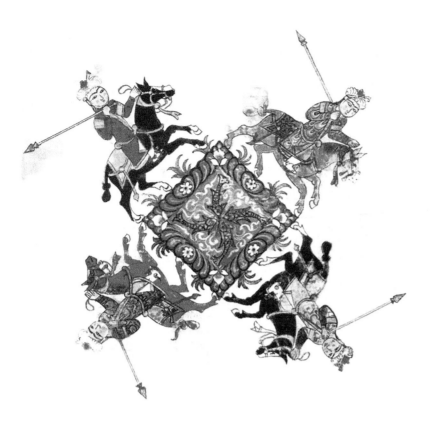

Mamālīk practising with lances, from the *Nihāyat al-su'l wa-al-umniyah fī ta'allum a'māl al-furūsīyah*, attributed to Muhammad ibn 'Īsā ibn 'Isma'īl al-Hanafī al-'Aqsarā'ī, c.1375–1400. There were several different techniques for a *mamlūk* to charge with the lance, including the *Khorasan*, *Damascus* and *Daylam* styles described in the *furūsiyya* manual *Munyatu'l-Guzāt*. All methods required 'a good horse, that is, one the legs of which are strong, which is well built and obedient and which is not hot-tempered or a balker' (Öztopçu 1986: 144). The process could be remarkably similar to that practised by Western knights: 'Damascus style tilting is carried out as follows: hold the lance with your right hand at a point one *arshin* [approximately 27in] from the butt, and press it in toward your armpit and hold it very close to the cheek of the horse. When you wish to tilt to your left side, move the lance over to your left side without moving your right hand from the place on the lance where you had been holding it, having passed it over the horse's head without letting the butt of your lance out of your armpit' (Öztopçu 1986: 141). There was also a keen appreciation of the use of the lance in other contexts, as well as parrying: 'One cannot parry (the lance in any way) in the Damascus (style) except from below upwards, because the butt of the lance is under his armpit. If your opponent comes (at you) holding his lance in the Damascus (style), be sure not to make any mistake when you parry, because if you make a mistake it is more difficult to bring down your lance from above, rather than to bring it upwards from below' (Öztopçu 1986: 172–73). (Pictures From History / Bridgeman Images)

Landing first at Acre the new army, commanded by a coalition of Frankish princes, the masters of the Military Orders (including the Teutonic Knights) and European kings, undertook a number of sorties against the possessions of the local Ayyubids; these excursions were for the most part desultory and inconclusive, and illustrated that, whatever benefits they may have brought, the crusade was still trying to find its feet. Jean de Brienne, King of Jerusalem and a man with a wealth of experience and adventure behind him, said:

> It is my opinion that we cannot accomplish very much at all against the Saracens in this land. However, if you consider that it would be a good idea, then I would gladly go into the land of Egypt, to besiege Alexandria or Damietta. If we are able to capture one of these cities, then I believe that we could, from this, have the kingdom of Jerusalem. (Quoted in Marshall 1994: 72)

The idea found favour quickly. Guillaume de Chartres, Grand Master of the Temple 1210–18, wrote to Pope Honorius III of how 'we have all now determined to undertake an expedition into Egypt to destroy the city of Damietta, and we shall then march upon Jerusalem' (quoted in Addison 1842: 154–55). To attack Egypt by sea meant securing a branch of the Nile to allow an invasion force to establish a stronghold from which to move upriver to Cairo. The western branch of the Nile was secured by Alexandria and the eastern branch by Damietta, described by the Patriarch of Jerusalem as 'the head and key of all Egypt' (quoted in Powell 1990: 138), and it was for this city that the Crusading fleet made upon its departure from Acre in May 1218. The chronicler Ibn al-Athīr noted how the first Frankish ships began arriving on 27 May

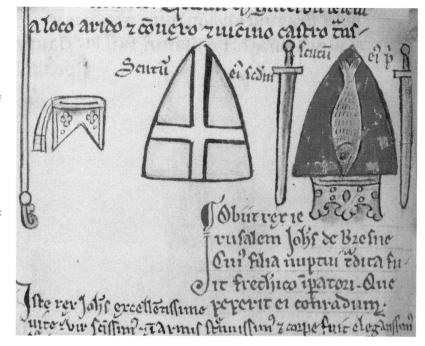

and anchored at al-Jiza. The Nile was between them and Damietta, and one of its branches flowed into the sea near the city. At this point a tall and well-fortified tower had been built by the Egyptians, with massive iron chains slung across the river to the walls of Damietta to prevent ships arriving from the sea from travelling up the Nile into Egypt. The Franks disembarked at al-Jiza, with the Nile between them and Damietta, and built a wall on their side and dug out a trench to defend themselves from attack. (Quoted in Gabrieli 2009: 152)

Al-'Ādil, brother of Salāh ad-Dīn and most powerful of the Ayyubid potentates, was in Syria at this time with his sons scattered among his possessions – al-Ashraf Musa in the Jazīra, al-Mu'azzam Sharaf-ad-Dīn in Damascus and al-Kāmil his viceroy in Egypt. The Syrian bishop Bar Hebraeus said of al-'Ādil that 'he was a very astute man, and one who nursed his anger, and took vengeance [on an offender] after a long period of time' (quoted in Budge 1932: 373). Such a view, while unflattering, admits the truth that to retain power amid the Ayyubid family a ruler had to have more than his fair share of ruthlessness and cunning. Although al-'Ādil had manoeuvred his sons into positions of power over those of his brother Salāh ad-Dīn, his age (he was 75 at the time of the invasion) and his growing ill health meant that the tensions that constantly pulled at Ayyubid unity were becoming more acute. Nevertheless the attack of the Franks on his most precious possession sparked al-'Ādil into raising an army, while his son al-Kāmil was set to contain the threat, arriving just to the south of Damietta

The misery of a siege. Though this image represents a classical siege of Jerusalem it conveys accurately enough the butchery, desperation and bloodshed that was the hallmark of many sieges of the time, especially that of Damietta. An estimated 50,000 people would die in Damietta, with the survivors numbering fewer than 10,000. (© The British Library Board, Egerton 2781 f. 190)

on 6 June. The chronicler Ibn al-Athīr noted: 'al-Kāmil … had camped in a place called 'Adiliyya [al-'Ādilīyah], near Damietta, and sent continuous supplies of troops to Damietta to prevent the enemy from landing on his territory' (quoted in Gabrieli 2009: 152).

By 29 May the crusaders had established their camp on a triangular stretch of land known as al-Jiza on the west bank of the Nile, opposite Damietta: 'an island, with the sea to the north, the river to the east, and the [al-Azraq] canal to the south and west of their camp' (Powell 1990: 147). The first step in assaulting the city would be to reduce the 'chain tower', defended by 300 well-equipped men supplied with stores of weapons including *naft* (Greek fire), that stood on a wooden foundation near the western bank of the river and which would be a tough nut to crack: 'from contemporary descriptions it is evident that the tower rose almost directly from the water and could be attacked only on the north side. The water to the west was too shallow for ships, and the chain obstructed an advance to the east' (Powell 1990: 141). The crusaders, denied the immediate leadership of Jean de Brienne whose ship had been delayed, elected Simon II von Saarbrücken to take matters in hand and launch an attack on the tower.

MAP KEY

1 27 May 1218: The Crusader fleet arrives off Damietta, and by 29 May the crusaders establish a camp on a triangle of land known as al-Jiza on the west bank of the Nile opposite the chain tower in the river and Damietta on the eastern bank of the river.

2 6 June 1218: On the orders of his father al-ʿĀdil, al-Kāmil encamps at Al-ʿĀdilīyah, allowing him to support Damietta and making a forced crossing of the Nile a dangerous proposition for the crusaders.

3 24 June 1218: The first assaults on the chain tower are rebuffed in short order. A more concerted attack on 24–25 August using a novel ship-mounted siege engine results in the tower's capture. Shortly afterwards al-ʿĀdil dies and is formally succeeded as sultan by his son al-Kāmil.

4 5 February 1219: Al-Kāmil, hearing word of a plot to unseat him, abandons his army which subsequently retreats. Being made aware that the sultan's troops have decamped, crusaders gain the eastern shore of the Nile without a fight and lay siege to Damietta proper.

5 29 August 1219: Stalemated at the city the crusaders

march to Fāriskūr to force a battle with al-Kāmil, which they lose, the Templars providing a crucial rearguard that helps keep the army intact.

6 8 November 1219: Damietta, starved and broken, falls as a consequence of an unguarded tower on its walls. Al-Kāmil subsequently retreats upriver to a more defensible position at al-Mansūrah.

7 17 July 1221: After much prevarication and political wrangling, the Crusader army moves out from Damietta, marching down the Nile to al-Mansūrah, encamping on the northern bank of the Ashmūn Tannāh canal c.30 July.

8 26 August 1221: The Crusader army, beset by the Nile's seasonal floods, harried by constant attacks, with its ships outflanked on the river and with al-Kāmil's brothers al-Ashraf and al-Muʿazzam moving to cut off its line of retreat, withdraws from its positions opposite al-Mansūrah.

9 29 August 1221: Pursued through waterlogged fields, the Crusader army is brought to heel at Barāmūn where it surrenders. Damietta is to be returned to the sultan.

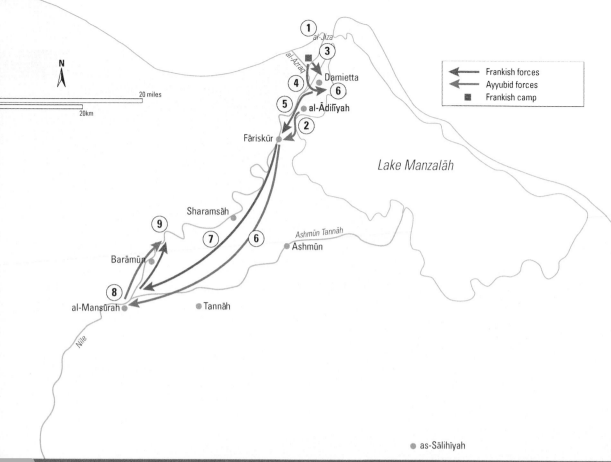

Battlefield environment

'Damietta! Renowned among kingdoms, very famous in the pride of Babylon, ruler of the sea, plunderer of Christians, seized in the pride of your persecutors by means of a few small ladders, now you are "humbled under the mighty hand of God"' (quoted in Peters 1971: 88). Thus spoke Oliver von Paderborn on the fall of the city, accurately reflecting its importance to the Ayyubids and to any invader who hoped to seize Egypt. Powell notes that 'The city of Damietta, according to the Arab geographer Yaqut, lay between Lake Manzalah and the Nile. To the north lay the Mediterranean Sea. Across the river was the Gizat Dumyat [al-Jiza], the peninsula of Damietta' (Powell 1990: 140). The city, a thrice-walled fortress (with a moat between the first and second walls) that impressed the crusaders with its size and sophistication, was shadowed by a tower near the western bank of the Nile: the chain stretched between one of Damietta's north-west bastions and the tower in the river 'served to interdict passage to the city or upriver to all but the merchantmen who obtained permission for the voyage, since the channel of the Nile to the west of the chain tower was not deep enough to permit access' (Powell 1990: 141).

Nothing remains of the original city of Damietta; in the wake of Louis IX's crusade – the third time that the city had been assaulted by Frankish invaders – the *mamālīk* tore it down and rebuilt it immediately to the south, with Baybars al-Bunduqdārī ordering the channel of the river be choked with rocks to deny future invaders the use of a navigable waterway. The coastline has also changed in the intervening centuries due to silting, the actions of the sea, and more modern human interference in the form of dam-building; thus the present coast may have added more than a mile of land to its medieval counterpart of 1218.

OPPOSITE A rather idyllic view of the Nile at Damietta that belies the generally urbanized environment that dominates the river's mouth and banks in this area. As a coastal city Damietta was subject to a more pleasant, temperate climate than that found in Egypt proper; the city's fertile surroundings impressed Oliver von Paderborn, who noted that 'because of its fishes, birds, and pastures, grain, gardens and orchards, it grew rich by tradition and by practicing piracy' (quoted in Peters 1971: 87). (Courtesy of Dr David Nicolle)

INTO COMBAT

Preparations for the assault were duly made by the Hospitallers and the highly capable Luitpold VI, Duke of Austria; launched on 24 June, the attempt was rebuffed in short order, with Oliver von Paderborn witnessing how 'the overjoyed Egyptians, mocking us violently, raised their voices, beating drums and sounding sackbuts' (quoted in Peters 1971: 64). The attackers constructed siege engines; Oliver von Paderborn proved to be something of an innovator as well as a chronicler, inventing a siege machine supported by a pair of ships that would allow the tower to be attacked more successfully from the river. Launched on 24 August, this fresh attack was driven home with vigour, allowing the Franks to seize the top level of the tower, which the defenders promptly set ablaze to force their attackers off. Despite their stubborn resistance it became clear, after a day and night of constant fighting that saw the garrison reduced to 100 men sheltering behind battered doors and walls, that the tower could not be held, so those that could not escape by swimming across the river to Damietta resigned themselves to their fate, surrendering to the duke of Austria on 25 August. The Egyptians quickly sunk numbers of ships in the throat of the river, ensuring that it would still be impassable for the Frankish fleet.

Such a victory for the Franks must have been a terrible blow for the defenders of the city, and a swift assault may have borne much fruit, but it was not to be; as Powell points out, many of the troops that had started out on the crusade now had to make for their homes before the seas became too dangerous to traverse, while at the same time the first of many reinforcing contingents began to arrive from England, France and Italy. Such shifts in personnel and leadership probably interfered with any plan to launch a quick assault on Damietta, and were to be a recurring aspect of the Fifth Crusade, doing it few favours. For Oliver von Paderborn the frustration of such inactivity was keenly, if not entirely fairly, felt: 'Although from that day the Babylonians were confused and terrified, and, it was thought, prepared for flight, our leaders fell into idleness and laziness according to their custom' (quoted in Peters 1971: 68). One of the changes in leadership that occurred at this time was the arrival of Pelagius, Cardinal of Albano and the papal legate. Though his initial influence on the crusaders was modest, his constancy

in the face of the arrival and departure of numbers of Frankish princes (especially Jean de Brienne) would lead to growing influence that many would see as detrimental, with his contemporary Roger of Wendover writing that Pelagius' presence in the Frankish army was 'more to the destruction of the Christians than to their support, as the ultimate issue of the business showed' (Wendover 1853: 134).

For the Egyptians the fall of the chain tower coincided with the death of al-'Ādil, as noted by Roger of Wendover: 'Also about this time, after the capture of the tower … Saphadin [al-'Ādil], the inveterate cause of evil days, and the disinheritor of his nephews, and the most wicked usurper of the kingdom of Asia, being affected internally with anguish of heart, died, and was buried in Hell' (Wendover 1853: 135). Ibn al-Athīr saw that 'His death lowered public morale for he was the real Sultan and although his sons bore kingly titles they were subordinate to his command, by grace of which they governed the various provinces' (quoted in Gabrieli 2009: 152). With al-'Ādil gone and 'succeeded by his son, Coradin [al-Kāmil], the unwearied imitator of his father's wickedness' (Wendover 1853: 135), his sons were free to make the most of their own principalities, perhaps at the expense of their siblings.

Seeking to try to drive the Franks from his lands or, at the very least, interrupt any attempts on their part to cross to the eastern bank of the Nile and lay siege to Damietta, al-Kāmil launched a number of sorties against the enemy camp. A strong surprise attack by 3,000 infantry was made on 9 October, but was beaten back with heavy casualties. Another assault was launched on 26 October specifically against the Templar camp, but this too was routed in short order by Frankish cavalry. During this time the crusaders, realizing there was no easy way across the Nile, took to deepening and widening the al-Azraq canal that lay to the south and west of their camp, and by so doing created a navigable waterway for their ships to move from the sea into the Nile below al-Kāmil's blockade. Grim weather and an outbreak of pestilence kept the Franks huddled in their camp over winter until finally, on 2 February 1219, they made a direct attack on the city of Damietta itself. The initial assault by the duke of Austria had some success, but poor weather again intervened, forcing the Franks back to their camp where they sat with their morale drowning in the rain and hail.

As the weather broke on 5 February Oliver von Paderborn noted how the Frankish army, instead of having to make another assault, found itself invited over the river by an 'apostate' who called to them '"why do you delay? Why are you afraid? Why do you hesitate? The sultan has gone away"' (quoted in Peters 1971: 74). A brief reconnaissance proved the man's words to be true – the whole Egyptian army had broken camp and left Al-'Ādilīyah quite empty. Though seeming a miracle to Frankish eyes, the truth was more prosaic. Al-Kāmil's position as sultan was far from secure; according to Ibn al-Athīr one of his *umarā*', Ibn al-Mastūb, 'hatched a plot with the other *amīrs* to depose al-Malik al-Kāmil in favour of his brother al-Malik al-Fā'iz ibn al-'Adil, and through him to control the whole country' (quoted in Gabrieli 2009: 153). Warned of the plot, but not knowing its extent or timing, al-Kāmil and a handful of men decamped to the village of Ashmūn Tannāh; the army promptly abandoned its supplies and followed its sultan. The next morning, puzzled by the absence of their foes, the Franks 'crossed the Nile unopposed, without any incidents or any need to defend themselves, and set foot on the soil of Damietta' (quoted in Gabrieli 2009: 153).

The Frankish army rapidly invested Damietta, but there was no quick breakthrough. Instead, al-Kāmil, whose position was so perilous, was rescued by his brother al-Muʿazzam of Damascus, whose opportune arrival with his army did much to stabilize the Ayyubid position. Jean de Brienne and the other leaders set about connecting the camps on each side of the river with a bridge and making the Damietta siege camp safe from attack. Now with his army at Fāriskūr a few miles to the south, al-Kāmil began to launch increasingly severe probes, culminating in a major assault on 31 March that was witnessed by Oliver von Paderborn: 'our enemies … collected a fearful and innumerable army of horsemen and foot soldiers and rushed upon us, invading our ramparts on all sides, especially the bridge of the Templars and the Duke of Austria … [they] leapt from their horses and fought savagely with the Christians' (quoted in Peters 1971: 78). The attack was beaten off, but the respite was short, with further assaults, large and small, launched by the Egyptians in the succeeding months.

For the crusaders this was a miserable time. The siege would have been a difficult endeavour even without the hunger and sickness that plagued the worn-down Frankish army, but it was made an altogether grimmer affair thanks to the fact that the Frankish camps had to defend against attacks of varying intensity from a significant enemy force only a few miles to the south. One such attack on 31 July came close to success; Oliver von Paderborn describes how the enemy

> brought forward all the power they could muster, and after many assaults, finally crossed the ramparts against the army of the Temple. Violently bursting the barriers, they put our foot soldiers to flight, to such an extent that the whole army of the Christians was then endangered … Fear welled up in the Christians, but … the Master of the Temple, with the Marshal and other brothers who were then present, made an attack through a narrow approach and manfully put the unbelievers to flight. (Quoted in Peters 1971: 79–80)

Jacques de Vitry witnessed the same event:

> The insulting shouts of the conquering Saracens were heard on all sides, and a panic was rapidly spreading through the disordered ranks of the whole army of the cross, when the Grand Master and brethren of the Temple made a desperate charge, and bravely routed the first ranks of the infidels. The spirit of Gideon animated the Templars, and the rest of the army, stimulated by their example, bravely advanced to their support … Thus did the Lord on that day, through the valour of the Templars, save those who trusted in Him. (Quoted in Addison 1842: 155)

As the weeks dragged by the Franks grew impatient, and on 29 August they made an attempt to finally eliminate the threat of al-Kāmil by marching the army, supported by a fleet of ships on the Nile, down to Fāriskūr to force a battle. The Egyptian army feigned a retreat, thus pulling the Franks further into dangerously inhospitable land where their cohesion began to fail in the face of Egyptian attacks, as noted by Oliver von Paderborn: 'the ranks were

One absq; tumultu + uiolenta depdatione. ut soli
filio dei uictoria ascribatur. Et cum caperetur au
tentus mitilis regis babilonis. n̄ fuit ausus more solito xp̄i
anos aggredi. Sj confusus aufugiens ipa castra combu
sit. Ep̄o itaq; duce milites xp̄i damietam ingressi. pla

Turris damiate

scattered except for a group of those whom obedience bound in military discipline. The knights of Cyprus, who were on the right flanks, showed their timidity to the Saracens as they made an attack from the side. The Italian foot soldiers fled first, after them horsemen of various nations, and certain Hospitallers of Saint John' (quoted in Peters 1971: 81–82). Things went from bad to worse as sections of the Frankish army melted away; others succumbed to heat exhaustion and thirst, with many captured or killed, but the Templars, together with most of the great men of the army, maintained their cohesion and provided cover for the retreating Franks. According to Oliver von Paderborn: 'The army of the Temple, which is usually first to assemble, was last to retreat. Therefore, when it arrived at last at our ramparts, it stayed without, so that it might bring those who were before it back within the walls as soon as possible' (quoted in Peters 1971: 83). The Templars lost 33 killed and captured, and the word in the camp was that 500 Frankish heads were presented to the sultan in celebration of the Egyptian victory.

Al-Kāmil had won a battle but little else. Damietta was still invested, and the Franks weren't going anywhere, while for the crusaders a similar sense of stagnation was unavoidable, as they were strong enough to defend themselves but not to convincingly defeat their enemy. With stalemate came a truce and talks, including the offer to return Jerusalem if the Franks would just go away. Powell notes that 'Without question, the sultan hoped to attain by treaty what he had failed to achieve in battle' (Powell 1990: 160), and though his offer of the holy city was certainly tempting there were too many issues on both sides, strategic and cultural, for a treaty to solve the impasse. The sultan remained in his tent, the Franks in their lines, and all continued as before for another month or so until, on 5 November, some Italian troops noticed that one of the city's towers was unguarded. Stealing across the walls they took the tower and with that, Damietta itself in 'a bloodless victory over a dying city' (Powell 1990: 162). Of the original 60,000 inhabitants, a scant 10,000 were left, wracked with disease and starvation. The defenders, outnumbered and without supplies, surrendered the city on 8 November.

For the Franks it was, according to Roger of Wendover, 'owing rather to a miracle than assistance from men, [that] the city of Damietta was taken and completely restored to Christian worship' (Wendover 1853: 136). Oliver von Paderborn says that upon the loss of the city 'the sultan himself, in confusion, burned his own camp and fled' (quoted in Peters 1971: 87), retreating from Fāriskūr up the Nile to the more defensible position of al-Mansūrah. His brother, al-Mu'azzam, left Egypt for Syria to engage in attacks on the Crusader States while the invaders of Egypt, secure in their new fortress, fell into plundering, politicking and planning. For the best part of two years the Franks remained at Damietta, unsure of the next move to make and hampered by the absence of strong leadership, with Jean de Brienne having left to attend to a dynastic matter that turned into an excuse for him to stay away, and Frederick von Hohenstaufen, now the Holy Roman Emperor Frederick II, still eagerly awaited, and still absent. Pierre de Montaigu, Grand Master of the Temple 1218–32, wrote how 'After the capture of Damietta, our army remained for some time in a state of inaction, which brought upon us frequent complaints and reproaches from the eastern and the western Christians' (quoted in Addison 1842: 157). The papal legate Pelagius, who was by this

ab eqs   dano q̃ n̄o longe xanoỹ fuuʃ tentoꝛuʃ manebat

time the de facto commander of the crusade, found himself in a situation where the need to do something to stop the ever-changing factions of the Frankish army from falling apart was hampered by the confusion over when – if ever – the promised leaders and their reinforcements would arrive. In the circumstances the suggestion of Ludwig I, Duke of Bavaria, to make an attack on the sultan's camp at al-Mansūrah seemed like a good one; it would get the army moving again, but would not, in theory, be a commitment on the scale of an attack up the Nile to Cairo. With the eventual return of Jean de Brienne with fresh troops shortly before the army was due to march, the prospects seemed auspicious, despite the Nile's approaching flood season.

Finally, on 17 July 1221 the Franks, with 1,200 knights including the Military Orders plus Turcopoles, cavalry, 4,000 archers and an unknown number of foot soldiers, moved out of Damietta and began the march south. The reaction among the Egyptians was one of near panic, with Ibn al-Athīr noting how al-Kāmil wrote desperate letters to his brothers in Damascus and the Jazīra 'imploring their help and begging them to come in person, or at least to send him their troops' (quoted in Gabrieli 2009: 154), while Cairo's inhabitants were evacuated in a state of terror at the prospect of the approaching Franks. Turkish cavalry began to harass the advancing army with raids, showering them with arrows in attempts to provoke a foolish reaction, but the Franks refused to engage, pressing ahead towards their goal, apparently heedless of the tactical limitations of the environment they were marching towards. Not only was the river expected to flood within days, but the crusaders were marching straight 'into a bottleneck created by the Nile and the canal [Ashmūn Tannāh] from al-Mansūrah to Lake Manzalah' (Powell 1990: 188).

Ibn al-Athīr notes that 'The two armies encamped facing one another but separated by a tributary of the Nile known as Bahr Ashmūn [Ashmūn Tannāh]. The Franks attacked the Muslims with catapults and ballistas, and were, like everyone else, sure that they would gain control of the whole of Egypt' (quoted in Gabrieli 2009: 154–55). Such certitude might have been found at the start of the endeavour, but not now; having marched themselves into a perfectly disastrous position, the crusaders discovered that al-Kāmil had cut off the Nile as a line of retreat, while the armies of his brothers al-Ashraf and al-Mu'azzam were moving themselves between the Frankish army and Damietta in an attempt to block retreat by land. Pierre de Montaigu, Grand Master of the Temple, wrote of how

the annual inundation rapidly increased, and the sultan, passing his galleys and armed boats through an ancient canal, floated them into the Nile below our positions, and cut off our communications with Damietta … Nothing now was to be done but to retrace our steps. The sultans of Aleppo and Damascus, the two brothers of the sultan, and many chieftains and kings of the pagans, with an immense multitude of infidels who had come to their assistance, attempted to cut off our retreat. At night we commenced our march, but the infidels cut through the embankments of the Nile, the water rushed along several unknown passages and ancient canals, and encompassed us on all sides. We lost all our provisions, many of our men were swept into the stream, and the further progress of our christian warriors was forthwith arrested. The waters continued to increase upon us, and in this terrible inundation we lost all our horses and saddles, our carriages, baggage, furniture, and moveables, and everything that we had. We ourselves could neither advance nor retreat, and knew not whither to turn. We could not attack the Egyptians on account of the great lake which extended itself between them and us; we were without food, and being caught and pent up like fish in a net, there was nothing left for us but to treat with the sultan. (Quoted in Addison 1842: 157–58)

A traditional village on the Nile. Such places, rarely recorded on any map, would always suffer if a campaign or *chevauchée* came their way. This description from the *Chanson des Lorrains*, though talking of wars in Europe, nevertheless gives a good impression of the mundane misery the passage of an army caused: 'The march begins. Out in front are the scouts and incendiaries. After them come the foragers whose job it is to collect the spoils and carry them in the great baggage train. Soon all is tumult … The incendiaries set the villages on fire and the foragers visit and sack them … Money, cattle, mules and sheep are all seized. The smoke billows, flames crackle. Peasants and shepherds scatter in all directions' (quoted in France 1999: 71). Such a fate would have been common enough for the small villages and hamlets in the path of Pelagius' army. (Courtesy of Dr David Nicolle)

Ibn al-Athīr notes the despair that wracked the Franks: 'When they realized that they were completely surrounded, that communications were very difficult and death was gnashing its teeth at them, they lost heart, broke their crosses, and their devil abandoned them' (quoted in Gabrieli 2009: 155). Unable to advance or retreat, with great loss of supplies and mired in mud and water, there was nothing left for the Frankish army to do but hope for merciful terms. They bought their escape with the return to the sultan of Damietta, a city that he would have had some difficulty in retaking by force, and by their ignominious departure from his lands.

A great endeavour lay in ruins. What had promised so much with the capture of Damietta was squandered in delay and finally drowned in the flooded banks of the Nile. The Templars had fought with distinction, their courage and professionalism saving the day more than once, but it wasn't nearly enough. Confused as to its purpose and hindered by a shifting leadership of variable quality, the Frankish army was a victim of its own folly more than their enemies' skill. Al-Kāmil, safe from further immediate depredations at the hands of the Franks, now only had to fear his erstwhile allies, his brothers al-Mu'azzam and al-Ashraf, as the incestuous cruelty of Ayyubid family politics once again reasserted itself. Such machinations ensured that this would be a febrile region for the next 20 years, though al-Kāmil – and especially his successor as-Sālih – would try to mitigate such uncertainty by building up their corps of *mamālīk*. It had always been hard to find substantial numbers of Turks to bring into the sultan's service, but the gradual spread of the Mongols to the east was breaking apart empires old and new, flooding the slave markets with many potential recruits from the best Turkic lands, and displacing others, such as the Khwarezmians, into a rapaciously predatory, mercenary life.

La Forbie

1244

BACKGROUND TO BATTLE

'This melancholy battle then, so ruinous and disgraceful to the Church of Christ, took place under an unhappy star, between Ascalon and Gazara, on Saint Luke's Day' (Wendover 1853: 226). The 'unhappy star' that shadowed La Forbie had been some time in coming, and was a combination of Frankish political and military weakness, Ayyubid familial rivalries, and the fitful, slowly expanding ripples of disruption caused by Chinghis Khan's Mongol expansions. At first this distant thunderclap was barely heard on the soft shores of the Mediterranean, but soon enough 'a report of the inhuman Tartars, and of the destruction that they spread everywhere, pervaded not only the countries of the east, but the inland regions, and even the western kingdoms, so as to reach all the countries of the world, and alarm them exceedingly' (Wendover 1853: 220). The Khwarezmians, a Turkic people from the southern shores of the Aral Sea, had seen their empire entirely destroyed in less than two years (1219–21) by the advance of the Mongol armies, resulting in the migration of significant bands of their people to the west, in search of new pastures and opportunities. The account of the arrival of the Khwarezmians in the Latin East given in the *Rothelin Continuation* is pregnant with foreboding:

> [The Mongols] destroyed the kingdom of Persia. Out of that land they drove another sort of people who were called Khwarazmians and belonged to Babylon

The Church of the Holy Sepulchre at Jerusalem. The church, built by the Emperor Constantine in the 4th century, was supposedly constructed over the hill of Calvary and the tomb in which Jesus was buried, making it probably the most sacred of all spaces in Christendom. As such it was a natural place of refuge for those Christians of Jerusalem who had not fled by the time the Khwarezmians finally took the city, and the outrage felt in response to its subsequent desecration is easy to understand. Often damaged by fire, earthquake and invasion both before and after the Khwarezmians, the church has been rebuilt and restored many times. This image, taken by Auguste Salzmann, shows the church as it looked in 1854. (Metropolitan Museum of Art, www.metmuseum.org)

and the law of Muhammad. These could not find any nation of their own law who would receive them, because of their great wickedness and great cruelties, and they travelled on till they came to the sultan of Babylon [as-Sālih]. The sultan refused to give them a home in his own land, but granted them the holy city of Jerusalem and the holy Promised Land where Christians were living. He urged and ordered them to go there and promised them faithfully that if they did, he would support and help them with all his power. (Quoted in Shirley 1999: 63)

Political expediencies aside, the Ayyubids held much the same opinion of the Khwarezmians as did their Frankish foes, al-Maqrīzī commenting that they were 'a people whose lives were passed in war and plunder' (al-Maqrīzī 1848). The Crusader States of Syria and Palestine into which the Khwarezmians would come were, in the early 1240s, enjoying a period of relative prosperity. Jerusalem had been won back in 1229 through the diplomacy of Emperor Frederick II and the ruthless pragmatism of the Egyptian Sultan al-Kāmil; the treaty had displeased the Syrian Franks (who feared the Hohenstaufen Frederick's growing influence in their lands) and scandalized many in the Muslim world. The return of the holy city, albeit with its defences still in ruins, presaged a short period of growth in the Latin East, with the gradual reacquisition of lost lands as a result of the Baron's Crusade (1239–41) and Ayyubid political disunity, leaving the Frankish kingdoms on what seemed to be the cusp of a renaissance of sorts.

Such a renaissance was, however, balanced on the edge of precarious circumstance. The Sultan of Egypt, al-Kāmil, died in 1238, sparking a civil war that was driven by grimly grasping Ayyubid family politics. His son as-Sālih had, by hook and nefarious crook, managed to succeed to the throne of Egypt, but lost Damascus to his uncle as-Sālih Isma'il (hereafter Isma'il) in the process. The Frankish states, through self-interest and an inability to avoid the gravitational pull of Ayyubid infighting, had made common cause with Isma'il of Damascus against the new Egyptian leader when war came again in the spring of 1244, and thus became another faction in the seemingly endless

quarrels between members of the Ayyubid family. Khwarezmian mercenaries had been used by as-Sālih during his wars in Syria, where many of them had remained, causing constant anarchic misery throughout the land with their rapacious ways. So it was that, as this new war intensified between as-Sālih and his uncle Isma'il, the Egyptian sultan called upon Berke Khān, leader of the Khwarezmians, to lead his freebooters south into the Jordan Valley and meet up with his own forces at Gaza near the border with Egypt. The *Rothelin Continuation* noted how the Khwarezmians 'burst suddenly into the Christians' land by Safed and Tiberias, and the Christians had heard nothing of their coming. Then they overran and plundered the land. They made several strong attacks on the city of Jerusalem, where at this time the ramparts were few and lacked any crenellation' (quoted in Shirley 1999: 63).

The Khwarezmians, according to the Master of the Hospitallers at Jerusalem, spread like a stain throughout the land as they 'occupied the whole surface of the country in the furthest part of our territories adjoining Jerusalem, and had put every living soul to death by fire and sword' (quoted in Paris 1852: 498). Together with the masters of the Hospitallers and Templars, Robert de Nantes, Patriarch of Jerusalem, had made some small effort to bolster the city's defences by hastily rebuilding some of its defensive walls and strengthening its garrison, but these august men 'did not themselves dare to remain there' (Runciman 1994: 187). The majority of the Christian population found themselves abandoned to their fate, terrified and at the mercy of a savage foe, as noted by the Master of the Hospitallers at Jerusalem: 'these perfidious Choermians came in great force and surrounded the Christians ... making violent assaults on them daily ... and harassing them in various ways, so that, owing to these attacks, hunger, and grief, they fell into despair, and all by common consent exposed themselves to the chances and risk of death by the hands of the enemy' (quoted in Paris 1852: 498–99). The people fled the city hoping to find refuge in Joppa, but few would survive the journey. The *Rothelin Continuation* recounts that a scant '300 reached Christendom, and these were in a pitiable condition' (quoted in Shirley 1999: 64).

MAP KEY

1 Spring 1244: As a result of internecine familial politics the Ayyubids of Damascus, Homs and Kerak start a war with the Ayyubid Sultan of Egypt, as-Sālih. They persuade the Latin states to join them in their endeavour, agreeing to combine forces at Acre over the summer; meanwhile as-Sālih, to mitigate the forces assembling against him, pays Berke Khān's Khwarezmian mercenary tribes, around 10,000 strong, to invade Palestine from the north.

2 June 1244: The Khwarezmians ravage northern Palestine, taking Tiberias and then Nablus; their numbers are too great for any single army, either from Damascus, Homs, or of the Franks, to be able to put a stop to their depredations.

3 c.1 July: The Khwarezmians arrive in the vicinity of Jerusalem, raiding the surrounding lands and attacking the city. By 11 July they have breached the walls, but the Citadel resists their assaults.

4 August: Sultan as-Sālih sends a 5,000-strong force, mostly comprised of *mamlūk* cavalry and commanded by Rukn ad-Dīn Baybars al-Sālihi, to Gaza to defend Egypt's frontier and await their Khwarezmian allies.

5 23 August: The fall of Jerusalem. With no prospect of aid and under a promise of safe-conduct, the garrison of the Citadel surrenders. The garrison and the majority of the Latin population of the city flee to Joppa, but most are slaughtered in a series of raids and ambushes, only 300 or so gaining safety. The Khwarezmians loot and destroy many Christian holy sites in the city, massacring the remaining priests and civilians alike.

6 4 October: Setting out from Acre the allied forces of the Christian princes, in concert with the *umarā'* of Damascus, Homs and Kerak, march to intercept and destroy the Khwarezmians, who have continued south towards Gaza.

7 16 October: The allies meet at Ascalon to hold a council of war; al-Mansūr Ibrāhīm, *amīr* of Homs, suggests caution but is overruled by the pre-eminent Latin prince Gautier de Brienne and also by Robert de Nantes, Patriarch of Jerusalem.

8 17–18 October: The allied army marches from Ascalon and attacks the Khwarezmians and Ayyubids near the small village of La Forbie (Harbiyah), a few miles to the north-east of Gaza. The Franks engage the Egyptian Ayyubids on the right flank, their allies from Homs and Damascus in the centre and Kerak on the left, facing the Khwarezmians. Al-Nāsir's men from Kerak crumple quickly, leaving the Khwarezmians to overwhelm the centre, gradually destroying all opposition. The remaining soldiers of Homs and Damascus flee the field; the Khwarezmians turn to attack the Franks who are still heavily engaged against the Egyptians – the Latin army, caught between the two great cavalry forces, is destroyed, its remnants fleeing back to Ascalon.

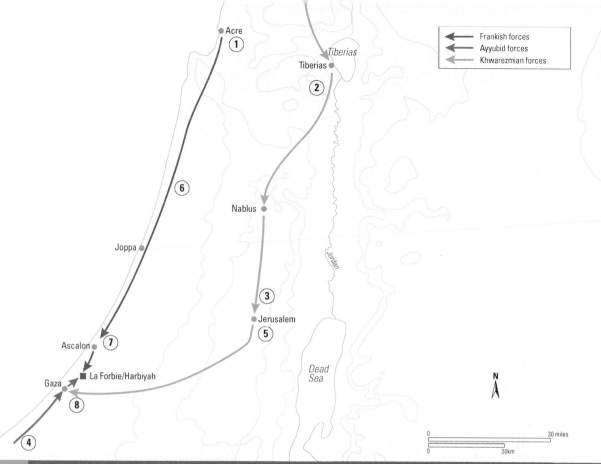

Battlefield environment

Gaza was built upon a low hill near the coast, with the village of La Forbie (Harbiyah) situated a mile or two to the north-east of the town on the wide plains that are prevalent in that direction. The temperature at the time of the battle would have been moderate, falling as it did in autumn, but summers were hot and dry, rainfall was very scarce, and there were few sources of fresh water.

The lands around Gaza were relatively sparse, with areas of gently rolling low hills and wide open fields. Taken by the Franks from the Fatimids in 1100, the town was initially insignificant in the crusading era despite having flourished in earlier centuries, but its position – astride the *via maris*

(Mediterranean coastal road) from Palestine into Egypt and beyond that all of Africa – meant it was well positioned for overland trade routes, not to mention strategically important for both the Fatimids and later the Ayyubids of Egypt, as well as the Crusader States whose southern bulwark it formed through most of the 12th century. The Templars built a castle there in 1149 but the town, falling to Salāh ad-Dīn in the 1190s, had its fortifications deliberately destroyed. Nevertheless, it was a natural place for as-Sālih to send his army to guard against incursions from his familial enemies, as well as from his violently untrustworthy Khwarezmian allies.

OPPOSITE La Forbie is a lost battlefield, the land on which it sits having been fought over and redrawn many times. The area where the battle was probably fought is now overrun by the suburbs of the modern Gaza City in a confusion of roads, settlements and industrial parks, leaving almost no indication as to what the land was like in the 13th century. Fortunately an artist, David Roberts, captured a pastoral scene of the area (entitled *Gaza, March 21st 1839*) during an artistic tour he took of the Middle East in the 1830s that conveys an idea of a landscape that, when he painted it, hadn't changed a great deal since medieval times. (David Roberts, Library of Congress)

INTO COMBAT

The massacre of the Christians of Jerusalem as they tried to flee presaged the desecration of the city itself. The Khwarezmians, with no force to stop or threaten them, ran riot. Al-Maqrīzī described how when 'they had despoiled all the country near to Damascus they advanced to Jerusalem, took it by storm, and put all the Christians to the sword' (al-Maqrīzī 1848). In the face of Jerusalem's seizure and violation, of the massacre of her inhabitants, and of such wanton desecration of every aspect of Christian belief and belonging, Frankish vengeance was inevitable. The Master of the Hospitallers caught the mood: 'At length, as the intolerable atrocity of this great crime aroused the devotion of all the Christians to avenge the insult offered to their Creator, it was, by common consent of all, agreed that we should all, after asking assistance from Heaven, arrange ourselves in order, and give battle to these treacherous people' (quoted in Paris 1852: 499).

Jerusalem was poorly fortified and garrisoned, and the Frankish princes lacked the capacity either to improve the city's lot or to assemble a host to relieve its woes once it fell under the shadow of the Khwarezmian horde. As such, the stark reality of the military capability of the Crusader States was laid bare: they had the strength to defend their main lands and fortresses, but lacked the men and resources to do much else of note without help from the West – or their neighbours. To mount a serious attack upon the Khwarezmians the Franks would need the help of their nominal Ayyubid allies, principally the sultan of Damascus. According to the *Rothelin Continuation*:

> all agreed strongly that they could not fight the Khwarazmians on their own, being so few in number compared with the invaders. They decided unanimously to send the sultan of Damascus [Isma'il] and the sultan of Homs [al-Mansūr Ibrāhīm], who were bound to the Christians by truces promising them aid and defence of Christian-held lands against all kinds of people of their own law, to ask them to come and help the Christians against the Khwarazmians who had entered their land. Both these sultans promised upon oath to help them. (Quoted in Shirley 1999: 63)

Such alliances did not necessarily sit easily with Muslim or Christian alike, and Emperor Frederick II, who admittedly had his own more venal reasons for disliking such an accommodation, voiced what must have been a common enough sentiment:

> expecting to find faith in perfidy, using dishonest artifices, they united the sultans of Damascus and Crach [Kerak], not only different in faith, but discordant in interests also with them, to help them against the army of the Choermians and the sultan [as-Sālih], as if one should send for a quantity of oil to put out the fury of a raging fire. (Quoted in Paris 1852: 493)

For as-Sālih, the confusion and terror that the Khwarezmians brought to Palestine was nothing but good news, discomfiting as it did the Franks and their allies, his much-hated family. The Khwarezmian horde, estimated in the *Eracles Continuation* to number '20,000 mounted men at least' (quoted in Shirley 1999: 132), was a significant force of fast-moving cavalry – even if in reality the figure was more likely to be around 10,000 or so (the standing forces of all

Egypt were barely more than this). Having wrecked their way through Palestine and ridden roughshod over Jerusalem, the Khwarezmians moved off in the direction of Gaza to join forces with as-Sālih's *mamālik*. Al-Maqrīzī records how

> after this expedition they marched to Gaza, and deputed some of their principal officers to NedjmEddin [as-Sālih]. This prince caressed them much, had them clothed in superb dresses, and presented them with rich stuffs and horses of great value. He desired that they would halt their troops at Gaza, where he proposed making a junction of the two armies, promising to march them to Damascus. The troops of the sultan were soon [ready] to take the field, under the command of the emir RukneddinBibars [Rukn ad-Dīn Baybars al-Sālihi], one of his favourite slaves, and in whose bravery he wholly confided. (al-Maqrīzī 1848)

Catapult projectile from Montfort castle. Montfort (called Starkenberg – 'strong mountain' – by the Germans) was the headquarters of the Teutonic Order for over 40 years, beginning in 1229. The Teutonic Knights, officially known as Orden der Brüder vom Deutschen Haus der Heiligen Maria in Jerusalem ('Order of Brothers of the German House of Saint Mary in Jerusalem') took their initial inspiration from the Hospitallers, though their more martial proclivities were modelled after the Templars. Formally recognized in 1192 and formed into a military order in 1198, the Teutonic Knights would have a significant presence in most of the campaigns and battles that were endemic to the Latin East throughout the 13th century, including Damietta, La Forbie and Louis' fateful crusade of 1248–50. The projectile shown here was most likely hurled at Starkenberg by the besieging armies of Baybars during their attacks of 1266 or of 1271, when the castle eventually succumbed, forcing the Teutonic Knights to decamp to Acre. (Metropolitan Museum of Art, www.metmuseum.org)

In support of this plague of mercenaries as-Sālih had organized an army to move towards Gaza as promised, both to meet with them and probably also to ensure that such a wildly unpredictable element stayed out of Egypt. This army, numbering about 5,000 horse and some foot ('3,000 Turks', according to the *Eracles Continuation*), was led by a highly capable *mamlūk amīr* called Rukn ad-Dīn Baybars al-Sālihi (not to be confused with Baybars al-Bunduqdārī of later al-Mansūrah fame who would go on to become sultan), and was almost certainly made up in large part of picked *mamlūk* cavalry.

The Crusader States, so ineffective in the defence of the holy city, now drew their forces together around Acre, the largest such gathering since the catastrophe at the Horns of Hattin 57 years before. The Frankish contingent was led by the pre-eminent knight of the kingdoms, Gautier IV, Comte de Brienne, and also by Philippe de Montfort, Lord of Tyre and Toron 'who was the standard-bearer of the kingdom and commander of the advanced guard' (Paris 1852: 492). Other worthies included in the army were Robert de Nantes, patriarch of Jerusalem, the archbishop of Tyre and the bishop of Ramleh, as well as numerous men of high birth and influence.

The Military Orders, an ever more essential part of any Frankish force, contributed around half the army's knights as well as an unknown number of Turcopole cavalry, sergeants and foot soldiers. Armand de Périgord, Grand Master of the Temple, came with about 350 knights; Guillaume de Châteauneuf, Grand Master of the Hospitallers, brought over 300 knights (200 according to Emperor Frederick II); and the Teutonic Order, under the command of their marshal Conrad von Nassau, brought just over 400 knights. A further 600 knights drawn from the Crusader States and set to join the army at Joppa rode under the command of Philippe de Montfort, and there were additional contingents of knights sent from Tripoli and Cyprus as well. The total number of knights who would take the field stood at around 2,000, with the remainder of the army being made up from perhaps about 10,000 other troops, including sergeants, foot soldiers and crossbowmen. The armies of Damascus and Homs, numbering around 4,000 cavalry under the command of al-Mansūr Ibrāhīm (*amīr* of Homs), together with several thousand light cavalry (probably Bedouin in part) from the army of Kerak under their *amīr* al-Nāsir and his general Zāhir al-Dīn Sungur al-Halabi, joined forces with their Frankish allies at Acre.

On 4 October the combined army left Acre, marching along the coast road towards Ascalon where it would meet with Gautier de Brienne and the remaining Frankish contingents coming from Joppa. Al-Maqrīzī notes the significance of such an event: 'this was the first time the standards of the Christians, on which was a cross, were seen intermixed with those of Muslims' (al-Maqrīzī 1848). The Kerak contingent and al-Nāsir, a man who had no love for the Franks, rode somewhat apart from the main force on the left flank, though between the Frankish commanders and al-Mansūr Ibrāhīm there was perfect cordiality. Arriving at Ascalon the combined armies of Christian and Muslim Syria paused to take stock and consider the best approach to the next part of the campaign.

The opinion of al-Mansūr Ibrāhīm, the Sultan of Homs and a man who had bested the Khwarezmians twice before, was that the best approach was a defensive one, fortifying the camp and refusing battle; the Khwarezmians were not fond of assaulting fortified positions, and were by their very nature not suited to prolonged operations. His view was recorded in the *Eracles Continuation*:

> My lords, you are dealing with a large nation of foreigners who have no base here. This will make them desperate, and I strongly advise against battle. We should stay here, as we have plenty of food and will get more from Acre; they have very little food and are numerous, they cannot possibly stay long but will have to move on. All we need is for them to go away, and as they are foreigners without a base they will not be able to stand firm, they will destroy themselves and will have to go. (Quoted in Shirley 1999: 132–33)

His view was well argued and cogent, for he must have suspected that although as-Sālih would use the Khwarezmians in Palestine he would almost certainly block their entry to Egypt, forcing them back on their own very limited resources. Though there was much agreement with al-Mansūr Ibrāhīm's position among the Franks, a proportion of them, led by Gautier de Brienne, were in favour of a direct attack upon the Khwarezmian–Egyptian army, because 'their forces were superior in number [and] it was a glorious opportunity for destroying the Khwarismian menace and humiliating Ayub [as-Sālih]' (Runciman 1994: 189). Emperor Frederick II, in a letter to Richard of Cornwall, noted that Gautier was not the only author of Frankish impetuousness, for the Patriarch, Robert de Nantes, was just as eager for blood:

> For while love and what was due to faith animated the Christians who had survived the massacre made by the Choermians, to take vengeance for such a devastation and such a great disaster, at the very moment when the counsels of the leaders, and the wishes of every private soldier aspired to do something in reparation of that misfortune, The Patriarch of Jerusalem, hoping for himself to obtain all the glory of the victory, and looking on every other prince and sharer therein as unworthy to be associated with himself, began to preach the crusade of the Lord, aroused the spirits of those who heard him, and inflamed them with courage bordering even upon rashness. (Paris 1852: 492)

Whatever the truth of Gautier or Robert being the more forceful in the matter, it was the decision to attack immediately that won the day, described in the *Eracles Continuation* in woeful terms: 'Through hatred and envy amongst the Christians, through sin and misfortune, the worse plan prevailed, and so they set out from Ascalon at dawn on a Tuesday morning and rode to Gaza' (quoted in Shirley 1999: 133).

The Frankish–Syrian army moved towards the enemy forces drawn up on a sandy plain a few miles north-east of Gaza by a small village called La Forbie (Harbiyah). Emperor Frederick II in his letter to Richard of Cornwall lamented that 'without waiting for a favourable moment, that most important rule in war … the Christian army, composed of all kinds of foreign chivalry, threw themselves upon the abovenamed Choermians' (Paris 1852: 492). The Franks were on the right (western) flank; al-Manṣūr Ibrāhīm's men from Damascus and Homs formed the centre, while al-Nāsir and the army of Kerak formed the left (eastern) flank. The *Rothelin Continuation* notes that as 'the hosts of Christendom approached Gaza, they saw the Khwarazmians and the men of Babylon arrayed in their companies ready for battle. The Christians placed their own squadrons in such a way that the sultans of Damascus and of Homs would have to fight first' (quoted in Shirley 1999: 64–65). The Egyptian *mamālik* held the left of their line, facing the Franks, while the Khwarezmians were matched against Syrians in the centre and the men of Kerak on the right. According to Al-Maqrīzī, the battle was started by the Khwarezmians, who 'made the first onset' (al-Maqrīzī 1848), whereas the Master of the Hospitallers says, 'We accordingly attacked them, and fought without resting from early in the morning till the close of the day, when darkness prevented us from distinguishing our own people from our enemies; immense numbers fell on our side; but four times as many of our adversaries were slain, as was found out after the battle' (quoted in Paris 1852: 499). The *Rothelin Continuation* notes how the 'armies drew near and clashed, Saracens against Saracens. Neither side spared the other in the least, just as if they had not been followers of the same law' (quoted in Shirley 1999: 65).

The fighting resumed the following day, with a strong attack by the Khwarezmian–Egyptian army against the Syrians and Franks. According to the Master of the Hospitallers:

> On the following (St. Luke the Evangelist's) day, the Knights Templars and Hospitallers, having recovered breath, and invoked assistance from above, together with all the other religious men devoted to this war, and their forces, and the whole army of the Christians, in the Holy Land, assembled by proclamation under the patriarch, and engaged in a most bloody conflict with the aforesaid Choermians and five thousand Saracen knights, who had recently fought under the sultan of Babylon, and who now joined these Choermians. (Quoted in Paris 1852: 499–500)

The intensity of the Khwarezmian attack on the Syrian centre and left flank was bearing fruit, however. The Damascene troops crumpled and ran under the ferocity of the onslaught, with Zāhir al-Dīn's left wing following quickly thereafter, fleeing the field. Al-Manṣūr Ibrāhīm's army of Homs was all but annihilated, with Ibrāhīm escaping the field by the skin of his teeth along with a scant handful of survivors. Al-Maqrīzī comments on the collapse of the army of Kerak, noting that with 'Zahir, who commanded the left wing, being made prisoner, there only

Charging at La Forbie

Templar view: The army of the Franks combined with that of the Ayyubids of Damascus, Homs and Kerak had tarried only a single night at Ascalon. The Frankish forces, with the Military Orders at their heart, made up the army's right flank, and engaged the Egyptian Ayyubid *mamlūk* cavalry in a series of charges that became a vast mêlée. The *Eracles Continuation* described how at least some aspects of the charge degenerated, as the 'Christians began milling about, the squires and foot-sergeants pushed in amongst the ranks and the knights could not spur forward to get at the Turks' (quoted in Shirley 1999: 133). Cohesion in a charge was critical, with riders gathering speed until the point of impact and trying to keep pace with one another in a formation that was so closely packed that their knees would often rub together. It would seem that at La Forbie the charge opened up, some knights lagging behind while others ran too far forward, with successive lines (the sergeants and squires) becoming intermingled with the main line, thus negating their ideal role as a fresh force to exploit success or a covering force to mitigate defeat. Here the Templars, already ragged and spread out, make scattered contact with the counter-charging *mamlūk* line.

Mamlūk view: The favoured tactics of *mamlūk* cavalry – circling at the edge of an enemy's range, wearing him down with harassing showers of arrows and always dancing out of reach when such provocation became too much – was not the only string to their bow. Excellently trained in the use of the lance and sword as well as bow, *mamlūk* riders were not afraid of closing for the kill, their skills, armour, mounts and horsemanship making them the equal of the best that the Military Orders had to offer. The first line would be made up of their finest, most experienced troops, and it would often be salted with some of the army's most skilled horse archers whose role was to harass and kill enemy leaders and standard-bearers. Long hours of practice in the *maydān* would develop the *mamlūk* horseman's technique with the lance, and such training allied with intensive hunting and polo would develop his ability to handle himself in single combat or as a part of a larger body of horsemen. Here the *mamlūk* line charges into the Templars in what would quickly dissolve into a riotous mêlée which seemed to offer neither side, matched in numbers and skill, much of an advantage. The Franks, fully engaged with the Egyptian *mamlūk* force, may have held their own or even won the field if not for the collapse of their allies on the centre and the left, resulting in thousands of Berke Khān's mercenary horsemen wheeling about and crashing into their flank, the Khwarezmian hammer to the *mamlūk* anvil.

remained the Franks, who for some time defended themselves, but were soon surrounded by the Kharesmiens' (al-Maqrīzī 1848). The stark reality of the Frankish situation is made clear in the *Rothelin Continuation*:

> This left the Christians standing alone on the field of battle, and they were very few compared with their enemies. Vigorously the two forces attacked each other; very sharp and cruel was the encounter. It was hard to believe that so few could fight so well against so many unbelievers. Then the Khwarazmians and the men of Babylon made a joint attack and at last ours could not stand against such overwhelming numbers. (Quoted in Shirley 1999: 65)

The *Eracles Continuation* records the confusion such reverses had upon the Franks: 'the sultan of Homs and his Turks soon rode off the field and fled; they lost all their equipment. The Christians began milling about, the squires and foot-sergeants pushed in amongst the ranks and the knights could not spur forward to get at the Turks' (quoted in Shirley 1999: 133). The Master of the Hospitallers takes up the thread, noting how

> a fierce attack was made on both sides, as we could not avoid them, for there was a powerful and numerous army on both sides of us. At length, however, we were unable to stand against such a multitude, for fresh and uninjured troops of the enemy continued to come upon us, as they were ten times as numerous as we, and we wearied and wounded, and still feeling the effects of the recent battle; so we were compelled to give way, abandoning to them the field, with a bloody and dearly bought victory; for great numbers more fell on their side than on ours. (Quoted in Paris 1852: 500)

The *Eracles Continuation* is clear that the collapse and rout of the Frankish army was a punishment: 'Envy, pride and folly brought the Christians to this' (quoted in Shirley 1999: 133). The Master of the Hospitallers managed to find some glory in defeat:

> And we were so assisted by Him who is the Saviour of souls, that not a hundred escaped by flight, but, as long as we were able to stand, we mutually exhorted and comforted one another in Christ, and fought so unweariedly and bravely, to the astonishment of our enemies, till we were at length taken prisoners (which, however, we much tried to avoid) or fell slain. Hence the enemy afterwards said in admiration to their prisoners: 'You voluntarily threw yourselves in the way of death; why was this?' To which the prisoners replied: 'We would rather die in battle, and with the death of our bodies obtain glorification for our souls than basely give way and take to flight: such people, indeed, are greatly to be feared' (Quoted in Paris 1852: 500)

This 'terrible slaughter, and one to be lamented throughout all ages' (Wendover 1853: 226) led to the deaths or captivity of most of the Frankish army, including its commanders: 'the masters of the Temple and Hospital were both taken and led into captivity, and other brethren of the different orders ... and nearly all the nobles of the Holy Land, either fell in battle, or were oppressed in captivity by the Saracens' (Wendover 1853: 226). The Master of the Hospitallers gave a grimly succinct review of the disaster: 'In the said battle, then, the power of the

Roland trying to break his sword Durendal. From a stained-glass window at Chartres Cathedral, *c.*1220–1240. The reality of a crushing defeat like that delivered at La Forbie fitted within an established cultural tradition for the knights of the West. The *Chansons de Geste*, cycles of songs and stories mainly concerned with the legends of King Arthur, with the great deeds of classical antiquity, and with the trials of Charlemagne and his chief Paladin Roland, had been increasing in popularity for many years, dominating the cultural life of knightly Christendom. Within such stories defeat was not uncommon, with probably the most famous example being that of Roland, mortally wounded in battle with the infidels at Roncesvalles, who tries (and fails) to shatter his sword Durendal on a rock, the blade's resilience symbolizing the unbreakable strength of the religious icons that have blessed it and the faith that Roland has shown to his lord and his God. The groans of woe that wreathed the reporting of La Forbie were cast in a similar vein, with the deaths of so many knights upon the field tempered by the belief that such an end gave them at least the respect of their enemies and the glory of martyrdom. (Internet Archive Book Images)

Louis IX, King of France. Matthew Paris in his *Historia Anglorum* draws the scene where Louis, wracked with illness, hears of the disaster at La Forbie and rises from his sickbed to pledge himself to a new crusade to regain Jerusalem. Louis' reputation for saintly behaviour was well established before he embarked on his crusade, and his biographer, Jean de Joinville, leaves the reader in no doubt of his master's purity: 'The Holy King so loved truth, that, as you shall hear hereafter, he would never consent to lie to the Saracens as to any covenant that he had made with them … [also] in his words he was temperate; for on no day of my life did I ever hear him speak evil of any one; nor did I ever hear him name the Devil – which name is very commonly spoken throughout the kingdom, whereby God, as I believe, is not well pleased' (Joinville 1908: 139). Such a view needs to be tempered, of course, with the understanding that medieval piety did not deny a cruelly unswerving view of the 'enemies of Christ', be they Saracen or Jew, and in this regard Louis was still very much a product of his time. (© The British Library Board, Royal 14 C VII f. 137v)

Christians was crushed, and the number of slain in both armies was incomputable … of the Templars only eighteen escaped, and sixteen of the Hospitallers, who were afterwards sorry that they had saved themselves' (quoted in Paris 1852: 500). The Patriarch of Jerusalem, Robert de Nantes, managed to escape the field though wounded and only 'half-alive', supposedly fearing that the lord had considered him 'unworthy of martyrdom' (Lotan 2012: 58). His spiritual brethren were not so fortunate, with both the archbishop of Tyre and bishop of Ramleh among the dead. Philippe de Montfort also escaped, but many others (around 800 in total) were taken prisoner, including Gautier de Brienne (who would die in captivity in a fight over a game of chess) and the Constable of Tripoli. The dead numbered at least 5,000. Al-Maqrīzī notes the jubilation that such a crushing success engendered:

> The news of this complete victory arrived at Cairo … NedjmEddin [as-Sālih] was so delighted with it that he ordered public rejoicings to be made, and they were announced to the people by sound of drums and trumpets. The town and the castle of the sultan were illuminated for several nights. The heads of the enemies that had been slain in battle were sent to Cairo, and exposed on the gates of the town. The captive Franks arrived at the same time, mounted on camels: as a mark of distinction, horses had been given to the most considerable among them. ZahirbenSongour [Zāhir al-Dīn Sungur al-Halabi], one of the Syrian generals that had been taken, marched next, with the other officers of the Syrian army. They were paraded with much pomp through the town of Cairo, and then confined in prisons. (al-Maqrīzī 1848)

For as-Sālih the war was an unmitigated success. He had fought off the advances of his uncle, given the Franks a punishing lesson in Ayyubid family politics, and become master of more lands and fortresses throughout Palestine. His strength would grow and within a few years the cherished prize of Damascus would be his. The Khwarezmians, having served their master's purpose, were dismissed from his employ and barred from entering Egypt. 'Left to ravage Palestine and Syria with little coherent purpose, the rampaging savagery that had driven the Khwarizmians eventually burned itself out, and in 1246 they were roundly defeated by a coalition of Syrian Muslims' (Asbridge 2011: 629). Perhaps this was a just end for a people who had been the scourge of ally and foe alike. As for the *mamlūk amīr* who had brought him the great victory, Rukn ad-Dīn Baybars al-Sālihi, the reward was his sultan's growing envy and distrust, leading to his imprisonment and death a scant two years after the battle.

For the Franks, the short and terrible campaign had severe consequences. The calamity of La Forbie bled the Frankish armies white and cut a swathe through the Levantine aristocracy, leaving many Frankish princes shaken and fearful of the future. And yet, as with Hattin so many years before, the resounding echo of such a disaster for Christendom would awaken another wave of crusading zeal in the West. For Hattin the clarion call had been answered by Richard Cœur de Lion; this time the mantle would fall on a young man whose piety was matched by his vigour – Louis IX, King of France.

al-Mansūrah

1249–50

BACKGROUND TO BATTLE

The character of the Seventh Crusade, an undertaking that had on the face of it the capacity to make a radical impact on the Latin East, was set by its chief proponent, Louis IX, King of France. According to Bar Hebraeus,

> Ridafrans [Roi de France], one of the kings of the inner countries of the Franks, went forth with a mighty collection of people, horsemen, and footmen, and soldiers, and mighty men of war, and they sailed on the sea in great ships and in vessels which were filled with an endless amount of gold and silver, and weapons of war, and provisions. And the earth quaked at the sound of them, and it was reported that they were prepared to go forth to Egypt. (Quoted in Budge 1932: 414)

Having taken the cross in 1244 after surviving a grievous illness, Louis' desire to make his mark was probably driven to some degree by the grim news of the turmoil of La Forbie, but also by a sincere religious devotion that 'manifested [as] a deep and unflagging adherence to the ideals of crusading at a time when it had attained its fullest spiritual crystallisation' (Housley 2008: 579). He had the desire and, with the wealthy and powerful state of France at his command, the means. That his objective would be Egypt was never in any real doubt. The Egyptian Ayyubids, ruled by the increasingly frail Sultan as-Sālih, were both the 'richest and most vulnerable' (Runciman 1994: 216) of the Ayyub

states. The same approach had failed with the ignominious collapse of the Fifth Crusade, and the brief diplomatic successes of Emperor Frederick II had been ground into the bloody dust at La Forbie, but the French monarch was set on his course.

In his mid-thirties, Louis was 'a tall, slightly-built man, fair-haired and fair-skinned, perpetually suffering from erysipelas and anaemia; but his character never lacked strength' (Runciman 1994: 214). His piety, often a thing of show easily put on and off by many great men of that age, was genuine and well recognized within his own lifetime, and he had a strong reputation throughout Europe as a diplomat and an exemplary Christian monarch. With him would go his brothers Robert d'Artois, Alfonse, Comte de Poitiers (to bring reinforcements once the campaign was under way), and Charles, Comte d'Anjou, together with a large number of great men (including Hugues IV, Duc de Bourgogne and Pierre de Bretagne – also known as Pierre de Dreux – both cousins of the king) and their retinues of knights, men-at-arms and retainers.

Louis proved to be adept at marshalling his forces: 'None of the earlier expeditions was as well organized or financed, none had a more inspiring leader, none had a better chance of success' (Strayer 1969: 487). Preparations were thorough, with considerable financial planning (including help from a none-too-willing Church) married to consistent and thoughtful logistics, including the preparation of a special harbour of embarkation, Aigues-Mortes, as well as the purchase and hire of ships and the laying-in of stores both in France and at the army's staging post, Limassol in Cyprus. This was all to support an army of 15,000 men (2,500–2,800 of them knights, as well as 5,000 crossbowmen) embarking from France, in addition to contingents that would join the king at Cyprus, swelling the ranks to around 25,000 in total. Included in these were a contingent of Hospitallers led by their Grand Master Jean de Ronay, 300 English knights led by Sir William II Longespée and 300 Templars with the Grand Master of the Temple, Guillaume de Sonnac, at their head. The number of sergeants, squires and other troops (probably including Turcopole light cavalry and crossbowmen) is not recorded, but they must have made up a notable proportion of the French king's force.

The army left France from Aigues-Mortes and Marseilles in the summer of 1248, with the king's contingent reaching Limassol on the southern coast of Cyprus on 17 September. As the rest of the army arrived together with the contingents from Europe, the Military Orders and other Syrian lords, Louis took stock and was persuaded to wait until after the turbulent winter storms before commencing his assault into Egypt. There was also a degree of diplomatic friction between Louis and de Sonnac, which was instructive; the king's assumption that his decisions took precedence over those of his fellow

A Turkish horse archer engages his pursuers with a Parthian shot. To be on the receiving end of an attack by Turkish mounted archers was a trying experience. Aleppan chronicler Ibn al-'Adim describes how at the battle of Balat (1119) 'the arrows were like locusts because of the vast quantity of arrows which fell onto the horses and men' (quoted in Hillenbrand 1999: 514), a fact echoed by Ibn al-Qalanisi in his description of the same encounter, noting how eyewitnesses 'saw some of the horses stretched out on the ground like hedgehogs because of the quantity of arrows sticking into them' (quoted in Hillenbrand 1999: 514). The effect was much the same for the crusaders of the 13th century, with the French knight Jean de Joinville speaking of how at al-Mansūrah 'it chanced that I found a Saracen's gambeson lined with tow: I turned the open side towards me and made a shield of the gambeson, which did me good service, for I was only wounded by their darts in five places, and my horse in fifteen' (Joinville 1908: 196). (Internet Archive Book Images)

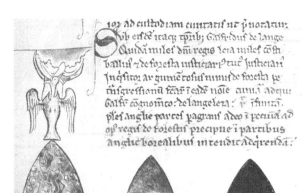

caption: The arms of some of the lords who fell in Egypt. The illustration, from the *Chronica Majora* by Matthew Paris, shows the arms of some of the notable men who fought in Louis' crusade. From left to right: the arms of Sir William II Longespée, with two hands above issuing forth from a cloud and holding a dove (honouring his brutal end in the street-fighting at al-Mansūrah, where he was apparently hacked to pieces); the lord of Saint-Omer; the lord of Ghent; the comte de Boulogne; the king's brother Robert, Comte d'Artois (with a black bird symbolizing his soul); and Raoul de Coucy. The inversion of the shields lets the reader know that the holders of such arms are dead. (© The British Library Board, Royal 14 C VII f. 148v)

crusaders was not automatically shared – certainly not by the Templars, who had over a century of experience and autonomy in the region. The individual viewpoints and egos of the men that made up the leadership of Louis' force mattered; such self-sufficiency of opinion and strength of character would be a major factor in the fate of the impending campaign.

The Muslim world that Louis IX was setting out to attack was not what it once had been. 'Saladin's empire had been divided among heirs who hated one another as only relatives can hate' (Strayer 1969: 489), and the internecine politics, backbiting and ruthless self-interest that were the hallmarks of most Ayyubid interactions had taken their toll. By the time the threat of another Frankish invasion was becoming clear, the position of the Egyptian Ayyubids was weak, in large part due to the failing health of Sultan as-Sālih. By most accounts a sour and solitary man whose demeanour wasn't improved by his chronic illnesses, he relied heavily upon his wife, his household staff and his *mamlūk* commanders to keep things together. The sultan's son and heir, Tūrānshāh, was far away in Mesopotamia and hadn't graced his homeland in years.

Despite the querulous nature of its sultan the forces that opposed Louis were still significant: strong bodies of well-trained cavalry, including the sultan's own Bahriyya *mamālīk*, were complemented by cadres of *halqa* (professional soldiers), foot and mounted auxiliaries (including Turcoman mercenaries), and irregulars drawn from Arabic tribes such as the Bedouin. The febrile nature of the Ayyubid political landscape ensured that most of these troops – and certainly their commanders – had seen battle and knew their business well.

With diplomatic endeavours coming to nothing and the gradual improvement in the weather, Louis' army gathered itself to set out for Egypt, with the port of Damietta at the mouth of the Nile as their first target. Almost as soon as his forces began embarking they were scattered by storms, the bad weather hampering Louis' eventual departure from Limassol until 30 May, and even then forcing him to let the bulk of his army follow on as best they could. Even so the king forged on, arriving off Damietta on 4 June 1249, ready and eager for war.

MAP KEY

1 5 June 1249: Louis' army lands on the beaches at Damietta and wins a fierce skirmish with the city's defenders led by one of as-Sālih's most senior *umarā'*, Fakhr ad-Din.

2 6 June 1249: Gripped by panic at the sight of Fakhr ad-Din's retreat, Damietta's garrison flees in the night. Louis enters the city unopposed.

3 6 June 1249: Hearing of the disaster at Damietta, as-Sālih breaks camp at Ashmūn and retreats to al-Mansūrah, approximately 35–40 miles south-west of Damietta, arriving there on 9 June.

4 20 November 1249: After a delay of five-and-a-half months awaiting reinforcements and for the annual summer floods of the Nile to abate, Louis' army begins a slow march towards al-Mansūrah; as-Sālih dies on 22 November, causing additional stress among the Ayyubids.

5 21 December 1249: Louis' army arrives opposite al-Mansūrah at the fork of the Nile and the Ashmūn Tannāh and spends the next six weeks trying to force a crossing of the canal in the face of stiff Ayyubid resistance.

6 Dawn, 8 February 1250: Shown a secret ford by a local Bedouin, Louis' army begins to cross the Ashmūn Tannāh; Robert d'Artois at the head of the army's vanguard of 600 knights (including the Templars) rides roughshod over the Ayyubid camp and charges into al-Mansūrah, where almost the entire force is massacred by the Bahriyya and Jamdāriyya *mamālīk* commanded by Baybars al-Bunduqdārī.

7 Afternoon, 8 February 1250: Louis' army, half on the north bank of the Ashmūn Tannāh and half on the south, fights a desperate battle against severe Ayyubid attacks, but manages to consolidate and defend its position.

8 5 April 1250: Louis' army, having wasted away for nearly two months, falls back towards Damietta. The retreating crusaders are harried by Ayyubid forces who catch up with them at Fāriskūr on 6 April, encircling and annihilating them. Only a small number, including the king himself, are taken for ransom.

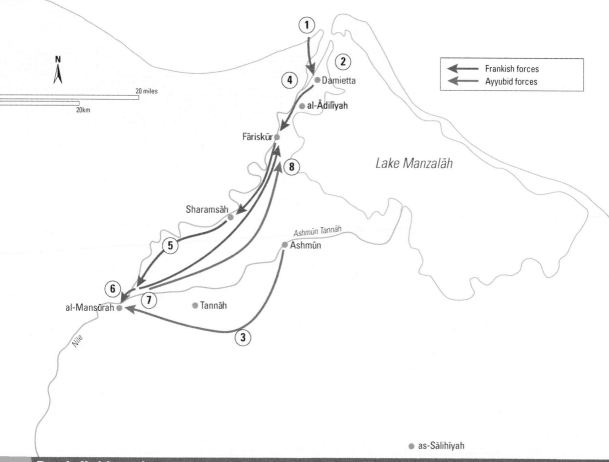

←	Frankish forces
←	Ayyubid forces

Damietta

al-Ādilīyah

Fāriskūr

Lake Manzalāh

Sharamsāh

Ashmūn Tannāh

Ashmūn

al-Mansūrah

Tannāh

Nile

as-Sālihīyah

Battlefield environment

As the crusaders marched up the Damietta tributary of the Nile towards al-Mansūrah, the lands through which they passed were relatively verdant and lush. Though all Egypt has a desert climate the lands of the delta, and especially those close to the coast, are more temperate; by the time Louis left Damietta in November 1249 the heat would have caused little hardship, though the nights would be cool and occasionally cold. Bar Hebraeus noted how, after the shocking fall of Damietta, as-Sālih 'went and encamped at a place which is called Mansurah, where there are dense plantations of trees' (quoted in Budge 1932: 414).

Al-Mansūrah itself was primarily a military camp that had been established by the sultan al-Kāmil in 1219 at the height of the Fifth Crusade. It had grown in the succeeding years and was now the main fortress south of Damietta, interrupting the passage of any invaders who would wish to march down the Nile to Cairo. Ibn Wasil described how 'the town stood on the eastern bank of the Nile, facing Jarjīr, with the canal of Ashmūn Tannāh dividing it from the peninsula on which Damietta is situated' (quoted in Gabrieli 2009: 169). Wasil described the Ashmūn Tannāh, the tributary from the Nile to Lake Manzalāh, as 'a small canal with a few narrow fords' (quoted in Gabrieli 2009: 171), though it was deep and dangerous enough to prevent any successful crossing by those who didn't know where those narrow fords were.

OPPOSITE This picture shows a waterway to the east of al-Mansūrah, providing a good example of the sort of landscape, rich with vegetation and spotted with trees, that would have greeted Louis' army as it marched up the Nile. The modern town of Mansoura is built over the ancient town and the location of the battle that defined it, effectively obliterating the site, though the location, at the junction of the Nile and a re-engineered canal that leads to Lake Manzalāh, remains the same. (Courtesy of Dr David Nicolle)

INTO COMBAT

Sultan as-Sālih had made Damietta defensible, or so he thought. The town had held out against the Franks for over a year in his father al-Kāmil's time, after all. Fakhr ad-Din, his venerable and trusted commander, was given responsibility for the defence of the town that was freshly garrisoned by Kinanites (Bedouin esteemed for their fighting qualities) as well as by Fakhr ad-Din's own troops. The sultan settled down upriver with his main force at Ashmūn on the Tannāh tributary, about 20 miles south of Damietta.

For Louis and his advisors, the decision was to attack at the first opportunity the day after their arrival – Saturday, 5 June 1249. The first landings were conducted by Lord Everard de Brienne and Lord Jean de Joinville (the author of *Vie de saint Louis*) in shallow boats, bearing them to the shore in the company of the king's barge: Louis, ignoring the pleas of his councillors that his place was aboard his flagship the *Montjoie* until the outcome of the landing was known, 'leapt into the sea, all armed, with his shield at his neck, and his spear in his hand, and was one of the first to reach the shore' (Joinville 1908: 136). There they were met by a strong force of cavalry:

> so soon as these saw us land, they came toward us, hotly spurring. We, when we saw them coming, fixed the points of our shields into the sand and the handles of our lances in the sand with the points set towards them. But when they were so near that they saw the lances about to enter into their bellies, they turned about and fled. (Joinville 1908: 174)

Fakhr ad-Din launched further attacks, but they were uncoordinated and haphazard, and failed to cause any real distress to the growing number of troops on the beach. Casualties were disproportionately high for the Muslims, with as many as many as 500 soldiers and two *umarā'* among the dead, while according to a letter sent by Guillaume de Sonnac, the capture of Damietta was achieved with the loss of only a single life among Louis' men. The French king's red tent was pitched on the shore in full view of the enemy, who were apparently disheartened both by the ever-increasing size of the Frankish army before them and their knowledge of their own sultan's frailty. Fakhr ad-Din marched his troops away almost immediately; that night 'God struck terror

Storming ashore. A letter from John Sarrasin in the *Rothelin Continuation* gives a good account of the landing: 'As we came in to land at least 2000 Turkish cavalry rode into the sea to encounter our men, and many on foot waded out as well. Our men, and the knights too, saw this as they stood armed in the boats, and … leapt fully armed into the sea … Then our crossbowmen renewed their efforts and shot so fast and so thick that it was a wonder to see' (quoted in Shirley 1999: 86). (© The British Library Board, Royal 20 D I f. 34v)

into their hearts' (Gabrieli 2009: 168) and the Kinanite garrison followed Fakhr ad-Din's example and fled Damietta, together with almost the whole civilian population, leaving the city open and mostly undamaged, and the bridge to the eastern bank of the Nile intact.

When as-Sālih heard of what had happened he had the entire Kinanite garrison hanged to a man, though he could not afford to spread his displeasure to Fakhr ad-Din or his men who, according to the chronicler al-Maqrīzī, would not have stood for any such treatment; by now loyalty to the clearly dying sultan was at best nominal among his *umarā'*. With Damietta gone as-Sālih had no choice but to withdraw his main force to al-Mansūrah where he arrived on 9 June, fortifying the area in anticipation of the victorious Franks. According to Ibn Wasil, 'The wall facing the Nile was rebuilt and faced with a curtain wall, galleys and fire-ships brought up, loaded with ammunition and troops and anchored under the wall, and uncountable numbers of irregular infantry and volunteers for the Faith flocked to Mansura' (quoted in Gabrieli 2009: 169–70).

For Louis and his men the almost immediate fall of Damietta was akin to a miracle. The *Te Deum* was sung and the king's army settled into the town and its environs, making the most of the hordes of supplies that had been assembled by the previous occupants in expectation of a significant siege. Historian Joseph Strayer notes that, with the Ayyubid forces retreating in demoralized confusion an immediate assault by Louis' army might have been decisive, but it was not to be. Louis was an excellent administrator but he lacked the incisive quality of a good field commander; and though the campaign's strategic objectives – the destruction of Egyptian Ayyubid power and the return of Jerusalem – were clear enough, the practical steps by which these were to be achieved were developing in tandem with the campaign.

Louis' decision to stay at Damietta was due to three factors: he was still awaiting the arrival of his brother Alfonse, Comte de Poitiers, with reinforcements; the Nile was on the verge of its annual flood, making any immediate campaigning fraught with logistical problems; and there was disagreement as to where the next attack should be made. The majority of the king's counsellors were for an assault on Alexandria, believing that it would secure their hold on the coast and provide a significant harbour for resupply; but Robert d'Artois vehemently disagreed, insisting that the only way to secure victory was to strike at the heart of the enemy's power, de Joinville recording his opinion that 'if you wanted to kill the serpent, you must first crush its head' (Joinville 1908: 180–81). Robert's argument won the day, and when the comte de Poitiers arrived with the promised men and equipment on 24 October the king's host made preparations to move.

The five-month sojourn in Damietta, during which time Louis had time enough to appoint a bishop as well as have his wife bear him a son, did his force few favours. The high morale that suffused the crusaders slowly dissipated in the indolence of the hot summer months, aided by an outbreak of disease and shortening rations. In addition, there were constant raids and assaults upon Damietta and the army's encampment, encouraged by the sultan's promise of a gold bezant for every infidel's head delivered to him. There was also the temptation of an act of diplomacy in the form of the exchange of Damietta for Jerusalem, though the king never gave the offer much consideration; In hindsight it might seem rash of Louis to reject such an opportunity, and perhaps it was, though there is little doubt that his

Baybars

Born north of the Black Sea into a Kipchaq Turkish tribe, al-Malik al-Zāhir Rukn al-Dīn Baybars al-Bunduqdārī (1223–77) would rise from humble beginnings to become the terror of the Crusader States, the man who blunted the seemly unstoppable Mongol incursions into the Fertile Crescent, and the greatest of the Bahrī Mamluk sultans. The ever-expanding Mongol threat from the east drove him – like many of his countrymen – into service with the Islamic states to the south, as generations of Turks had done before him; around 1242 Baybars was sold as a slave into Egypt, where he had the good fortune to be a part of as-Sālih's drive to expand his mamlūk forces. He was sent to the island of Rōdah on the Nile where as-Sālih had built a fortress where his mamālīk could train and reside.

Apparently demonstrating great skill at arms, especially with a bow (his sobriquet 'al-Bunduqdārī' means 'the pellet-bowman'), Baybars, after his training and manumission, became one of the Bahriyya (literally 'of the river') mamālīk, the sultan's own troops. His first major success came at al-Mansūrah; the sultan had died in November 1249 and his heir, Tūrānshāh, was far away in the Jazīra, so the amīr Fakhr ad-Din effectively took over only to be cut

down and killed in the first flush of the Frankish attack on the Ayyubid camp. Baybars, in command of the Bahriyya mamālīk quartered inside al-Mansūrah, took the situation in hand, ensuring that the rampaging crusaders would get in to the town but not out of it, sealing off the exits and falling upon them with a vengeance.

Once Tūrānshāh had arrived, Baybars was one of the mamālīk (some accounts say the very mamlūk) who deposed and killed him, though he soon fell foul of Aybak, the first of the Mamluk sultans, and fled to Syria where he remained until the new sultan, Qutuz, brought him back into the fold. The timing was auspicious; a powerful Mongol army was engaged by Mamluk forces at Ain Jalut on 3 September 1260, only a few months after Baybars had returned, and his notable role in that great victory was a significant factor in what happened next. Expecting to receive the domain of Aleppo from Qutuz in recognition of his proven prowess, Baybars was snubbed, presumably because the sultan feared his growing reputation and corresponding ambition; accounts note how Baybars responded, ramming a sword through Qutuz's throat while they were out hunting, taking the sultanate for himself in the process.

conviction and zealous nature would balk at taking by means of diplomacy that which he felt he had the divine right to seize by force. Thus it was that Louis' army, somewhat blunted by a humid and worrisome summer, set out for al-Mansūrah on 20 November.

For the Egyptians, the start of the crusaders' march was married with the grim omen of their ruler's death. Sultan as-Sālih, withering on the vine for many weeks, finally succumbed to his collection of illnesses on 22 November, though at first there were few who knew about it. His widow Shajar al-Durr, in concert with Fakhr ad-Din, moved with a secrecy matched only by speed to ensure that the sultan's will would be maintained, even if the sultan was no longer around to help. Al-Muʿizz Aybak, one of the most senior of the Bahriyya mamālīk, was immediately despatched to find as-Sālih's heir Tūrānshāh and bring him home, while Fakhr ad-Din took control of the army. How many of these manoeuvrings were carried out in naked self-interest as opposed to a selfless desire to keep up the morale of the nation is debatable, but despite their best efforts the news of as-Sālih's death started to seep out, bolstering the spirits of the infidels and casting another unsettling shadow over the people of Egypt.

Louis' march south, slow and deliberate, followed closely the route of the Nile, allowing the army to move its baggage and supplies in concert with the main force. The crusaders suffered from near-constant harassment by numerous cavalry skirmishers and Arab irregulars as they pushed south, and though Louis, with conservation of his strength in mind, had ordered one and all to refuse engagements, there were occasions when such restraint proved too much, even on one occasion for the well-disciplined Templars:

Guillaume de Sonnac

Guillaume de Sonnac (*c*.1200–50) was a man of education and standing, having enjoyed a career in the Order in France, running the Commandery at Auzon by the age of 24 and rising to become Preceptor of Aquitaine by the time he was nominated to become Grand Master in 1247. Born sometime around 1200, Guillaume was a good example of the changing nature of recruitment into the Templars – a change that was driven by the secular world's evolving view that gentility was something every aspirant to knighthood must possess – in which the provable nobility of one's lineage was becoming a prerequisite to joining, and which presumably made a material difference to one's advancement through the Order henceforward.

An important man in Western Europe's most powerful state, Guillaume de Sonnac was well used to moving in august circles, and he must have mastered the practicalities of high politics, financial management and diplomacy during this period. He brought such expertise with him to the Latin East after his appointment to lead the Order, though his impact on the affairs of that region were quickly overshadowed by Louis' approaching crusade, in which the Templars would inevitably play a significant part. All too often the Grand Masters who led the Order, including Guillaume de Chartres at Damietta in 1219 and Armand de Périgord at La Forbie in 1244, met their ends mired in blood, and for Guillaume the campaign in Egypt would have a similarly fateful outcome. One of the most senior men of the Crusade, he had a reputation as an intelligent and circumspect man, and most accounts agree that he tried to temper the headstrong attack of Robert d'Artois at al-Mansūrah that led to the destruction of the army's vanguard and over 280 Templars. He was one of the very few knights of any stripe – and almost certainly the most senior – to escape the massacre within the city's walls, though he was severely wounded by a blow to the face in the mêlée, as a result of which he lost an eye. In the wake of such a serious reverse Louis' attack stalled and moved to the defensive in the face of increasingly ferocious opposition. His army sat with its back to the Ashmūn Tannāh, enduring attack after attack over the next two days; this ordeal culminated in a sustained assault by the Egyptians that, though eventually repelled, cost Guillaume, still leading his knights on the field, his remaining eye as well as his life.

Now it happened that when the host began to move forward, and the Saracens saw that no attack was to be made upon them – and they knew by their spies that the king had forbidden it – they waxed bold, and attacked the Templars who formed the van; and one of the Turks bore a knight of the Temple to the earth, right before the horse-hoofs of brother Renaud of Vichiers, who was then Marshal of the Temple. When the marshal saw this, he cried to his brother Templars: 'Out on them for God's sake! I cannot brook this!' He struck his spurs into his horse, and all the host with him. The horses of our people were fresh, and the horses of the Turks already weary; and so, as I have heard tell, not one of them escaped, but all perished. Many of them had got into the river, and were drowned. (Joinville 1908: 181)

By 21 December Louis had reached the fork of the Nile and Ashmūn Tannāh rivers, on the doorstep of the Egyptian position: the crusaders had the eastern bank of the Nile on their right flank and the Ashmūn Tannāh to their front; the Egyptian forces were encamped on the southern shore of the Ashmūn Tannāh, as well as in al-Mansūrah itself. With no obvious way across the Ashmūn Tannāh, Louis decided to build a causeway to force a crossing; a laborious exercise in engineering that necessitated much work as well as the installation of various engines of war (18 in total) to defend against the Egyptian engines (16, according to Joinville) that were bent on hampering the French initiative: 'Fakhr al-Din initiated an incessant bombardment, "using relays of men day and night" to sustain a constant barrage of "stones, javelins, arrows [and] crossbow bolts [that] flew as thick as rain"' (Asbridge 2011: 500). The crusaders' efforts seemed less impressive: 'Our engines threw against theirs, and theirs against ours; but never did I hear tell that ours had done very much damage' (Joinville 1908: 183).

The pommel of Pierre de Dreux's sword from al-Mansūrah. Pierre de Dreux (c.1187–1250), Duc de Bretagne was a seasoned campaigner both in France and in Outremer, where he had been a notable figure in the Baron's Crusade a decade earlier. As such he rode in the vanguard with Robert d'Artois, and accompanied him through the gates of al-Mansūrah; unlike Robert (and almost everybody else), Pierre de Dreux managed to escape even though badly wounded by a sword-blow across his face. At some point in the battle he lost his sword – an act immortalized in a stained-glass window at Chartres Cathedral, though the details of the (no doubt fascinating) story have been lost. Pierre de Dreux fought on but was taken prisoner on 6 April 1250. He was ransomed but died at sea before he made it home. The pommel of his sword – with the arms of Pierre de Dreux on the obverse and a crusader's cross on the reverse – turned up in Damascus in the early 20th century, confirming at least part of the evidence of the Chartres window some 700-odd years earlier. (Metropolitan Museum of Art, www.metmuseum.org)

The causeway's progress was unimpressive and the pair of towers that had been built to aid in its construction proved a magnet for Egyptian engine attacks of every sort, including Greek fire, the effect of which was keenly felt by the defenders: 'The noise it made in coming was like heaven's thunder. It had the seeming of a dragon flying through the air. It gave so great a light, because of the great foison [abundance] of fire making the light, that one saw as clearly throughout the camp as if it had been day' (Joinville 1908: 186). Finally the battering of stone, bolt and flame bore fruit and the towers were wrecked, burned beyond repair, and with them went any realistic hope of continuing with the causeway. For six weeks the crusaders had been mired by the banks of the Ashmūn Tannāh, struggling and failing to engineer their way across the river, all the while under near-constant attack from engines of war as well as increasingly bold cavalry raids that gnawed away at their flanks. Spirits began to flag.

For such religiously disposed men the arrival of a 'Bedouin' who offered for 500 bezants to show them the location of a ford a little way downriver must have seemed a literal godsend. The king ordered his brother Robert d'Artois to make a surprise crossing of the Ashmūn Tannāh with a cavalry vanguard before daybreak on 8 February and hold the southern bank until the rest of the army could be drawn up to join with it. The vanguard, numbering around 600 horsemen, comprised a number of notable and trustworthy knights from the French contingents as well as the Templars and the English knights led by Sir William II Longespée. The behaviour of the vanguard was explicitly laid out by the king, according to the *Rothelin Continuation*: 'Above all, it was imperative that the entire strike force reach the south bank and regroup before any attack was mounted. With this in mind, Louis "commanded them all – great men and small – that no one should dare to break ranks"' (quoted in Asbridge 2011: 501).

Though there is some confusion in the sources as to the reasons for the conduct of Robert d'Artois, all agree that he was the main author of the calamity that was about to unfold. Aged 34, Robert (called 'the Good' by some) certainly seemed to exemplify some of the more unseemly traits of the knightly character, being quarrelsome and violent, as well as displaying hauteur that slipped with ease into arrogance and then hubris. The sense conveyed by the chronicler Matthew Paris is of a knight with a need to gorge himself on glory, no matter the cost. That such a man led the vanguard of Louis' army at a time when it was out of contact with the main body, unsupported by foot troops and with any potential withdrawal hampered by a river, did not bode well. No sooner was the vanguard across than Robert, seized by fervour for battle and heedless of the call of Guillaume de Sonnac to stop, pushed his contingent to the fore (the place normally taken by the Templars) and made for the Egyptian camp that lay by the south bank of the Ashmūn Tannāh. Unable to control him, the Templars, 'shamed if they suffered the count to outride them' (Joinville 1908:189), charged after him *en masse*.

The wild ride of Robert d'Artois was quick to bear fruit. The Egyptian camp was entirely unprepared for the assault that fell upon it; according to Ibn Wasil, Fakhr ad-Din 'was washing himself in his bath when he heard the cry go up that the Franks had taken the Muslims by surprise. Frenziedly he leapt into the saddle, without weapons or any means of defending himself, and a band of Franks fell on him and killed him – God have mercy upon him!' (quoted in Gabrieli 2009: 171). With their commander cut down (supposedly by two

Mamālīk training with swords, from *Nihāyat al-su'l wa-al-umnīyah fī ta'allum a'māl al-furūsīyah*. Loyal and brave, *mamālīk* were a proud *corps d'élite*, especially those within the sultan's own household, but proud troops have a sense on their own value and *mamlūk* loyalty was not slavish or unconditional. A *mamlūk* saw his duty as being to his master, not his master's family, heirs or state. For the Bahriyya *mamālīk* such specific loyalty was of great worth to their master, Sultan as-Sālih, but upon his death they had no reason to transfer automatically their fealty to his son Tūrānshāh, newly returned after many years in the Jazīra. He could have won them over and made them his own (the *mamālīk* of previous sultans were usually incorporated into the new sultan's household in some way), but as-Sālih's hapless heir, either through design or incompetence, alienated them completely by moving his own favourites into positions of power and ignoring the legitimate claims of the senior Bahriyya *mamālīk*. There was no binding cultural or social reason for the Bahriyya *mamālīk* to accept such treatment from a man to whom, as they saw it, they owed nothing, and so Tūrānshāh found himself set-upon, cut down and left in ignominy on a riverbank, dead for three days before anyone bothered to bury him. (Pictures From History / Bridgeman Images)

mighty sword-blows delivered by a group of Templars) and Franks wreaking havoc at every turn, the Egyptians broke and scattered, many heading straight for the town of al-Mansūrah. Robert, his blood up and his eye fixed on greater glory, refused to brook any counsel from Longespée or the Grand Master of the Temple; the chronicler Matthew Paris described him as 'bellowing and swearing disgracefully as is the French custom' (quoted in Barber 1995: 150) and damning the Grand Master for his cowardice. Guillaume de Sonnac replied, 'Neither I nor my brothers are afraid … but let me tell you that none of us expect to come back, neither you, nor ourselves' (quoted in Asbridge 2011: 502); and with that the charge continued on, into al-Mansūrah itself.

The Frankish attack and the death of Fakhr ad-Din had caused panic and rout, but the *mamālīk*, 'Bahrītes and Jamdarites' (Wasil, quoted in Gabrieli 2009: 172) quartered in al-Mansūrah and led by Baybars al-Bunduqdārī, quickly restored some degree of order. The knights and sergeants of the vanguard poured into the town and soon found themselves in winding, narrow streets with little room to manoeuvre, fighting in vicious desperation. Routes out of the town were quickly blocked off and the crusaders were beset on all sides by *mamālīk*: 'lions in war and mighty in battle, [they] rode like one man upon the enemy in a charge that broke them and drove them back. The Franks were massacred one and all with sword and club. The Bahrītes slaughtered them and drove them back through the streets of al-Mansura' (Wasil, quoted in Gabrieli 2009: 172). Sir William II Longespée was killed, as were the vast majority of the vanguard; of the Templars, who had numbered around 300 at the day's outset, fewer than ten survived (one of them being

Trapped in al-Mansūrah

Having overrun the Ayyubid camp at the Ashmūn Tannāh in a 'brutal riot' (Asbridge 2011: 502), the Templar knights followed the impetuous Robert d'Artois straight through the gates of al-Mansūrah in a pell-mell pursuit of the fleeing Egyptians, intent on routing the whole of the enemy's forces. Unknown to the (roughly 600) men who made up the vanguard, al-Mansūrah quartered the Bahriyya *mamālīk* led by Baybars al-Bunduqdārī, an up-and-coming man of formidable talent.

The knights of the vanguard poured into al-Mansūrah and almost immediately found themselves split up, riding through narrow streets and alleys that confused their sense of direction and gave them little room to manoeuvre. Baybars and the Bahriyya *mamālīk* slammed the gates of the city shut behind the Frankish cavalry and blocked roads and passageways out of the town with timber beams. Their quarry trapped, the *mamālīk* then turned to the grim task of hunting down and killing all the Franks they could find. Knights found themselves beset on all

sides by swords, spears and arrows, the choking closeness of the town denying them the chance to ride free or take full advantage of their mounted status. Guillaume de Sonnac, Grand Master of the Temple, whom the chronicler Matthew Paris described as 'a discreet and circumspect man, who was also skilled and experienced in the affairs of war' (quoted in Barber 1995: 149), had entered the town against his better judgement and was one of very few Templars (some sources say only two) who managed to cut his way to freedom, though he would lose an eye in the process. Here, an already wounded Guillaume, with the aid of a knight and a sergeant who has lost his horse, desperately fights off a determined attack by a throng of furious *mamālīk*.

For Robert d'Artois, Sir William II Longespée, their respective contingents of French and English knights, as well as at least 280 Templars, there would be no escape from al-Mansūrah.

Guillaume de Sonnac, who had lost an eye); and Robert d'Artois, architect of this bloody folly, either fled the town and drowned trying to escape across the river or, more likely, barricaded himself inside a house with some compatriots until it was stormed by *mamālīk* who cut them down to a man.

With his vanguard destroyed, Louis found himself in a precarious position. Now on the southern bank of the river, the king's contingent had to fight hard against wave after wave of resurgent *mamlūk* cavalry, fending off charges and enduring showers of arrows and bolts. The viciousness of the fighting was well appreciated by Jean de Joinville who, knocked from his horse and trampled, found himself in a ruined house with a small coterie of knights, fighting desperately against an enemy that even thrust lances at them through holes in the roof:

Knights fleeing, in a scene from the Morgan Picture Bible (French school, 13th century). The final retreat of the Frankish army was an ignominious mess, as described by Ibn Wasil: 'In the battle the Bahrite mamlūks of al-Malik as-Sālih distinguished themselves by their courage and audacity: they caused the Franks terrible losses and played the major part in the victory. They fought furiously: it was they who flung themselves into the pursuit of the enemy: they were Islam's Templars' (quoted in Gabrieli 2009: 173–74). (Pierpont Morgan Library, New York, USA / Bridgeman Images)

Then did my Lord Hugh of Ecot receive three lance wounds in the face, and my Lord Raoul; and my Lord Frederic of Loupey received a lance wound between the shoulders, and the wound was so large that the blood flowed from his body as from

A battle between knights and Saracens. The retreat to Damietta ended in bloody ruin at Fāriskūr, as recounted in the *Rothelin Continuation*: 'Great companies of Turks surrounded our men … From every quarter the Turks launched vehement attacks on them and many died on both sides … The king was taken, and his two brothers the counts of Poitiers and Anjou, also the count of Flanders, the count of Brittany, the count of Soissons, and many other leading men and sergeants whose names we cannot give' (quoted in Shirley 1999: 102). (© The British Library Board, Egerton 745 f. 5v)

the bung-hole of a cask. My Lord Everard of Siverey was struck by a sword in the middle of the face in such sort that his nose fell over his lip. (Joinville 1908: 191)

The Ayyubid regiments pressed home their attack, forcing the king and his troops back towards the river where the fight was carried on with sword and mace. The situation was grim: 'we saw … that the stream was covered with lances and shields, and with horses and men drowning and perishing' (Joinville 1908: 194). Louis himself nearly fell into the enemy's hands, as

six Turks had come to the king's bridle and were leading him away captive, and that he alone delivered himself striking at them great strokes with his sword. And when his people saw how the king was defending himself, they took courage, and many of them abandoned thought of taking flight across the river, and drew to the king's side to help him. (Joinville 1908: 194)

The battle was a sea of small skirmishes blending into one another, making up a larger tapestry that could have ended in disaster until 'as the sun was setting, the constable brought us the king's dismounted crossbowmen, and they placed themselves in rank before us; and when the Saracens saw them setting foot to

Louis IX in captivity. The Ayyubid victory at al-Mansūrah was a close-run thing from the perspective of the people of Cairo. The joys of al-Mansūrah would, in a matter of months, be surpassed by the complete destruction of the Frankish army and the capture of their king at Fāriskūr, a feat beyond the wildest hopes of most. (Internet Archive Book Images)

the stirrup of their crossbows, they fled and left us there' (Joinville 1908: 196).

Louis had a ditch dug and a rudimentary palisade thrown up, and built a pontoon bridge to his camp on the north bank of the river. His army endured raids and minor assaults over the next two days until, on the third day, the whole fury of the Ayyubid army was thrown against them. Wave after wave of attacks pressed the crusaders, many of whom were still bearing wounds from the battle three days prior – including de Sonnac, who received a mortal wound, probably from an arrow, that took his remaining eye. 'And you must know that behind the place where the Templars stood there was a space, the size of a journeyman's labour, so thickly covered with the Saracens darts that the earth could not be seen by reason they were so many' (Joinville 1908: 202–03). To the defenders the intense ferocity of the *mamlūk* attacks, captured in the *Rothelin Continuation*, made them appear to be men that 'hardly seemed human, but like wild beasts, frantic with rage … they clearly thought nothing of dying' (quoted in Shirley 1999: 98). Yet despite this Louis' army endured, and the attack abated.

Time and circumstance eventually achieved what the two great battles had not. Hammered by the events at al-Mansūrah, the king's army lacked the strength to push forward – but Louis still had too much pride to turn back. As the crusaders sat by the river disease began to take hold, the effects of which were compounded by a falling-off of supplies – unknown to the French, the Egyptians had moved some galleys up the Nile and were wrecking the invaders' all-too-fragile supply lines. By the beginning of April, Louis, surrounded by an army that was dying where it stood, bowed to the inevitable.

As the withdrawal from al-Mansūrah began the king's advisors, cognizant of the dangers ahead, suggested that he should take to a galley and make for Damietta ahead of the host, in part so that

> if any mischance happened to his people, he might thus, of himself, deliver them from captivity. And also, in particular, because of the condition of his body, which was afflicted by several diseases, for he had a double tertian fever, and a very sore dysentery, and the special sickness of the host in his mouth and legs. But he would listen to none, and said he should never leave his people, and should make such end as they made. (Joinville 1908: 136)

The retreat to the coast could not be conducted in anything like good order and the *mamālīk*, smelling blood, harried and hounded the disintegrating force every step of the way. On the following day, 6 April, the majority of Louis' army was brought to ground at Fāriskūr, encircled and summarily massacred. The king and some small number of nobles worthy of ransom were taken, with nothing but a few tattered remnants escaping to make it back to Damietta. The most pious of kings at the head of one of the best-organized and best-equipped armies of the age had failed utterly. 'Thus the failure of Louis contributed to the loss of confidence, the hesitations, and even the cynicism which weakened all later crusades' (Strayer 1969: 488).

Analysis

The Knights Templar and the Egyptian *mamālīk* were something of an anomaly for their time; both the Knights of Christ and their Turkish foes were thoroughgoing professionals in a recognizably modern sense, men who (generally) saw duty before glory, who trained both individually and as part of a group, and who had the discipline to function effectively within a clear hierarchy. The *mamālīk*, sometimes seen as the knights of Islam and even 'Islam's Templars' (Gabrieli 2009: 174) according to the chronicler Ibn Wasil, were not an Islamic form of Western knighthood. While such comparisons give a good sense of their martial prowess, they overlook the centuries-long distinctive culture and history that gave rise to the *mamālīk* of the Ayyubid period. They were a military elite like the Templars, but unlike them they were also culturally distinct from their masters and the people of the lands in which they lived; and though Muslim they were not chained by the fervour of faith, rather seeing the world through distinctively Turkish eyes.

The model of a knight sworn to God, eschewing worldly glory and pleasure for service and self-abnegation, was a new concept in the early 12th century, and one that developed great power very quickly. The reputation that the Templars won for themselves among both friends and enemies is testament to the seriousness with which they took their calling, for that is what such a life was. The Order showed a remarkable ability to rebuild itself, even after the most crushing of defeats, and its consistency and strength throughout the 13th century was a significant factor in the longevity of the Crusader States, beset as they were by a never-ending succession of enemies and circumstance. At Damietta, La Forbie and al-Mansūrah they evinced a consistent and unwavering commitment to the goals of their Order in particular and the armies of the Latin East in general. That each of these campaigns descended into ignominious failure was in spite of their contribution, rather than because of it.

Crossbowmen assaulting city walls. The eventual capture of Damietta caused widespread existential horror throughout the Ayyubid lands, as noted by Ibn al-Athīr: 'All the rest of Egypt and Syria was on the point of collapse and everyone was terrified of the invaders and went in anticipation of disaster night and day … If al-Kāmil had allowed them, they would have abandoned the country altogether, but impeded as they were they stood firm' (quoted in Gabrieli 2009: 154). The gift of such a success was not just in its strategic value, but in the enormous boost it gave to Frankish morale and the concomitant despair it engendered in the Egyptians. When compounded with the death of Sultan al-'Ādil and the ructions within the Ayyubid ranks, the failure of the Franks to strike home their advantage seems almost perverse. The decision to march on the sultan's camp probably came far too late, and certainly Pelagius and the other leaders made a monumental strategic error in continuing with their advance on al-Mansūrah after they had learned of the arrival of al-Mu'azzam and al-Ashraf, because at the very least such forces would negate any advantage the Franks might have gained through a victory at al-Mansūrah.
(© The British Library Board, Yates Thompson 12 f. 204)

DAMIETTA

The army of Egypt, with assistance from the forces of Damascus and the Jazīra, had shown courage and persistence in fighting the Franks, but at a strategic level it did little to stem the advance of the enemy until the final days of the campaign, and this failing must be laid at the door of the sultan. Al-Kāmil, a man who had no hesitation in trying to bargain his way to a peaceful life, had more than his fair share of luck in dodging the consequences of military inaction. Painful prevarication followed by impetuousness could characterize the Frankish army in the wake of its capture of Damietta, where some of the most frustrating aspects of medieval warmaking were on display for months to come. The observation that 'crusader leaders, raised in the chivalric code of individual valour, were reluctant to accept subordination to any single person' (France 2005: 71) certainly explains some of the problems under which the Frankish army laboured in Egypt. Leadership of the crusading army was split between Jean de Brienne, King of Jerusalem, the council of the army (which was composed of the leaders of the various contingents that made up that force, including the Grand Master of the Temple and the Grand Master of the Hospitallers), and the papal legate Pelagius of Albano. Ultimately, this was a feudal force drawn together from many nations that was the product of its time and environment, and as such it suffered inordinate stresses in trying to maintain a coherent character hundreds of miles from home, on the shifting sands of an enemy shore, for years on end. That it managed to remain a vital and critically dangerous foe to the Egyptians for so long was, in the circumstances, all the more remarkable.

LA FORBIE

That the Khwarezmians were able to ride though Palestine causing havoc wherever they went, seemingly immune from significant Frankish resistance, may give the impression that the forces of the Crusader States were weaker and more vulnerable than was in fact the case. It was certainly true that the Franks lacked the resources to field an army capable of defeating the Khwarezmians on its own, but the strength of the Frankish lands lay in their fortresses, and the trade that such establishments protected. Jerusalem, for all its symbolic importance, had seen most of its defences torn down and was vulnerably situated, making it a much easier nut to crack than most crusader strongholds. The city's ruinous fall was not a strategic problem as such for the Crusader States, but it was a grave insult that struck at the very heart of Frankish pride, and was also a direct challenge to Christian identity in the East. It would be unthinkable for the knights and princes of Syria, men motivated in large part by a personal prestige that was underpinned by Catholic righteousness, to let such a deadly calumny remain unanswered.

In deciding to treat with as-Sālih Isma'il of Damascus rather than as-Sālih Najm ad-Dīn Ayyūb of Cairo it seems – with hindsight certainly – that the crusaders backed the wrong horse. The Mongol incursions had allowed a far greater recruitment of high-quality Kipchaq Turks into *mamlūk* regiments, as well as forcing peoples like the Khwarezmians to sell their services to whomever would have them. Both *mamālīk* and mercenaries were costly, and as-Sālih, sitting at the heart of the richest province in the Ayyubid confederation, had the money that his relatives lacked. In addition, all the benefits that the Franks had accrued from their dealings with Isma'il (such as the return of Galilee and new religious rights in Jerusalem) were always tentative, in that what the sultan of Damascus gave, the sultan of Cairo always had the potential to take away if he so chose. Nevertheless, any Frankish alliance with Damascus, Cairo or any other Ayyūb province would probably have been a case of building upon shifting sands, as the mercurial and internecine nature of that family's politics allowed little room for consistency or trust.

Despite such political and strategic considerations, the Frankish defeat at La Forbie was not inevitable. Though the army was a cultural composite, it seems to have operated in relative harmony (with the exception of al-Nāsir of Kerak), and it was hardly unusual during this era to field ad hoc forces made up from different contingents of varying nationalities. The desire to seek battle in the face of the sensible advice from the sultan of Homs to wait their enemy out, whether driven by the Patriarch of Jerusalem or Gautier de Brienne, was probably heightened as a result of the Khwarezmian atrocities. The battle itself was a gamble, and a good example of why many military leaders of the time avoided such risks, where one could win or lose everything in a few hours. The forces were more or less evenly matched in numbers (15,000 or so each), which should have given the attackers pause for thought, especially considering they had no other advantage going for them such as surprise or good ground. It seems likely that the recent nature of the Frankish–Syrian alliance weighed against them when they were put to the test, though the sources are unclear on the matter. That the men of Homs fought well while those of Damascus and Kerak fled suggests the possibility of more serious fault lines within the Syrian forces, rather than with the Frankish–Syrian alliance overall.

AL-MANSŪRAH

At al-Mansūrah, 'Crusading heroism had won the battle, but chivalrous folly had already lost the campaign' (Strayer 1969: 501). As goes the glory, so must go the blame. Though his army was initially well prepared and thoroughly organized, Louis' inability to control his subordinates would cost him dearly. His choice of his brother Robert to lead the vanguard over the river was fateful; that his orders were disobeyed cannot have been such a surprise, as he must have known his brother's character to be excitable and hungry for the laurels that would accompany a great victory. It is worth bearing in mind, however, that – distinct from the Military Orders – Western armies were led by professional warriors, not professional soldiers; coupled with the egos and appetites that most significant men of the time displayed, it must have been extremely difficult for any commander to exercise his will effectively among such knightly and headstrong folk. Even the Templars, though led by a man who was apparently well respected for his experience and prudence, found themselves falling victim to hot-blooded impetuousness, either of their own or another's making.

The king also made several strategic errors of varying significance. The initial victory at Damietta may have been a remarkable opportunity, but the king had neither the experience to see this nor the incisiveness to make something of it. His use of the Nile as a supply line seems sensible, but its relative lack of protection was not; Louis did not seem to appreciate that his lifeline was vulnerable to enemy depredation. His actions at al-Mansūrah during the battles of 8 and 11 February 1250 were personally courageous and did a great deal to keep his army intact. The folly of his impetuous brother caused the loss of critically important troops, which was compounded by the intensity of the fighting in general. Here, in refusing to understand that his army lacked the strength to go any further against an enemy that, if anything was getting stronger rather than weaker, Louis doomed his men. He ignored the logical step to retire in good order to Damietta, instead opting to remain paralysed with indecision on the riverbank, sinking into the mire while the sinews that bound his host together slowly rotted away.

For his foes, there is some truth to Humphreys' assertion that 'the miraculous victories of 1221 and 1250 had been a very near thing indeed – gifts of crusader stupidity rather than Muslim military prowess' (Humphreys 1998: 3). The loss of Damietta after barely a day was potentially catastrophic, both to Egyptian morale but also the whole strategic defence of Egypt. The lack of any serious attempt to recapture or lay siege to the city may be due in part to as-Sālih's ailing health, but both at Damietta and later at al-Mansūrah the attitude of the Ayyubid army was defensive and reactive. They fought hard and well when battle was finally joined, and the consistency of their attacks in the days after the initial Frankish assault across the Ashmūn Tannāh certainly blunted the capability of Louis' army, as well, perhaps, as its hunger for more fighting. Nevertheless, it was Louis' failure to exploit the capture of Damietta, to control his brother, and to refuse to retreat after al-Mansūrah, that ruined his chance not just of victory but of escape.

A horseman fighting two foot soldiers. This offers a traditional view of the value of horse over foot, even if by the time this medal was minted in 1468 such a time had long since passed. Discovering the nature of foot troops in the crusading period isn't easy, as they were often overlooked by the sources, both in everyday life and battle. Such men – in the form of foot sergeants, spearmen, engineers, archers and crossbowmen – played a significant role in the endemic warfare of the Latin East. They would form tightly knit defensive walls behind which the mounted knights could shelter both while on the march and in the thick of battle; foot soldiers and engineers were essential in laying (or defending against) siege; archers and crossbowmen in particular had a vital role in keeping the mamlūk horse archers at a safe distance, and in providing cover for retreating forces, as so clearly demonstrated by Louis IX's corps of crossbowmen at al-Mansūrah. (Metropolitan Museum of Art, www.metmuseum.org)

Aftermath

After 1250 the Latin East seemed to be living on borrowed time. The Military Orders, especially the Templars, were as significant a presence as ever – even more so as more and more lands and fortresses were turned over to their protection as their erstwhile owners admitted that they lacked the men and resources to maintain them. The fervour of crusading that had reached its height at the start of the century was waning as the years passed by, bogged down by failure and disaster. Such detachment from the West left the Frankish kingdoms more vulnerable to the shifting sands of circumstance than ever before.

The Ayyubids, driven by a mixture of self-interest and fear, were not 'any more involved with the crusaders than immediate circumstances compelled them to be' (Humphreys 1977a: 3). This was not the case with their successors, for whom 'the army was the state' (Humphreys 1977b: 69); the rise of the *mamālīk* to the Sultanate of Egypt was a grim portent for the Crusader States and the Military Orders that were their strongest bulwark. The internecine confusion of the Ayyubid period would be replaced by a *mamlūk* ascendancy characterized by vigour and uncompromising ideas of expansion that had little regard for the dreams of Frankish princes. The Templars, still a force of military, financial and political power, could – and did – try to stand firm against this incoming tide, but they were far too few in number to brook its progress. The Crusader States were almost entirely defensive by this point, and without massive and consistent support from their cousins across the sea there was little they could do to counter the advances of a multitudinous, well-trained and motivated enemy.

The Mosque of Baybars in Cairo, by W.S.S. Tyrwhitt. The seeds of the Mamluk Sultanate were sown by as-Sālih, whose paranoia caused him to insulate his own *mamlūk* corps from the rest of the army while at the same time he expanded their numbers and power within his regime. (Internet Archive Book Images)

RIGHT The siege of Acre. The erosion of Frankish territory under the onslaught of Baybars had been drastic and irreversible. Finally the forces of Sultan al-Ashraf came to Acre in May 1291. According to Abu l-Fidā, the final assault came on 17 June that year: 'The Sultan forced all those in the towers to surrender, and they submitted to the last man, and to the last man were decapitated outside the city walls. At the Sultan's command the city was razed to the ground' (quoted in Gabrieli 2009: 207). (© The British Library Board, Royal 20 C VII f. 24v)

BELOW Templars being burnt at the stake. This image, taken from *Chroniques de France ou de Saint-Denis* (from 1270–1380), shows the grim end that awaited at least some of the Knights Templar. The Templars quickly fell foul of the French king Philippe le Bel (Philip the Fair), a man who, most likely in order to extirpate his vast debts to the Order, had them arrested, damned as heretics, and wracked with torture until they confessed to their supposed misdeeds, then publicly burned. (© The British Library Board, Royal 20 C VII f. 44v)

Baybars, the man who had exacted such a cruel price from Robert d'Artois' impetuousness at al-Mansūrah, would himself become sultan, shattering in turn Mongol armies and a series of Frankish strongholds. At times almost a personification of the growing *mamlūk* political and military hegemony, Baybars viewed the Crusader States with withering contempt, and his campaigns against them were implacable. Eighteen years after the failure of Louis' adventure another Frankish prince, Bohemond VI, ruler of Antioch, found his city the target of the sultan's ire. In a stark letter to Bohemond announcing his intention to wrest Antioch from Frankish rule, Baybars left no room for misunderstanding about what was to come:

If you had seen your churches with their crosses broken and rent, the pages from the false Testaments scattered, the graves of the patriarchs rifled, your Muslim enemy trampling down the sanctuary; had you seen the altar on which had been sacrificed the monk, the priest and the deacon, with the patriarchs crushed by disaster and the children of your kingdom enslaved ... had you seen these things, you would have said: 'Would that I were dust.' (Quoted in Hillenbrand 2007: 165)

BIBLIOGRAPHY

Medieval sources

A noted historian of Egypt, **al-Maqrīzī** (1364–1442) was born over a century after Louis' crusade, so his account of those events relies upon a variety of sources. His editorial judgement of the internal politics and motivations of the senior figures in the Muslim army is worthy of note.

The chronicler **al-Ansārī** (d. 1408) was an important man at the *mamlūk* court of the late 13th century who had considerable experience in war. As Carole Hillenbrand notes, 'There is no reason to doubt that much of the content of al-Ansari's treatise is relevant for an understanding of warfare in the immediately preceding centuries' (quoted in Scanlon 2012: 4).

Muhammad ibn ʾĪsā ibn ʾIsmaʿil al-Hanafī al-ʾAqsarāʾī (d. 1348), a man about whom little is known, wrote the *furūsiyya* manual *Nihāyat al-suʾl waʾ-lʾumniya fī taʿlīm ʾaʿmāl al-furūsīya* ('An end to the questioning and desire of learning the works of horsemanship'). Though not a *mamlūk* himself, his treatise on the arts of *furūsiyya* accords closely with many others, especially in its acknowledgement of the central relationship between horse and rider from which all else springs.

Ibn al-Athīr (1160–1233) was a general historian, his wide-ranging and famous work being *Al-Kāmil fī al-tārīkh* ('The Complete History'), written in 1231. Gabrieli says of him that 'His reputation among Orientalists has recently diminished, because of the free and tendentious use he makes of his sources, but the qualities that reduce his reliability as documentary evidence are those of an original thinker, outstanding among so many passive compilers of facts' (Gabrieli 2009: xvii).

Ibn Wasil (1207–98) was a contemporary chronicler of the late Ayyubid and early Mamluk period who had a distinguished diplomatic career and knew many senior people, such as Baybars, personally. His work, *Mufarrij al-Kurūb fī akhbār Bani Ayyūb* ('The Dissipator of Anxieties Concerning the History of the Ayyubids'), covers the Zangids, Salāh ad-Dīn and the crusades of the 13th century, for which he is one of the most important Arab chroniclers.

Jacques de Vitry (*c*.1160–1240) was elected bishop of Acre in 1214 and made Patriarch of Jerusalem in 1239; he played an important part in the Fifth Crusade. His unfinished work, *Historia Hierosolymitana*, as well as his letters, give a first-hand insight into the moral and religious imperatives that drove the Franks. As such, his views are cast in strongly religious and providential terms.

Jean de Joinville (1224–1317), an active participant in the Seventh Crusade, wrote his impressions of Louis' adventure shortly after its conclusion, though their revision and inclusion in his memoirs would not happen until he finished them in 1309 at the age of 85, over 50 years later. He writes, according to Marzials (translator of the 1908 edition), 'as an old man looking lovingly, lingeringly, at the past – garrulous, discursive, glad of a listener' (Joinville 1908: xxvii). As an eyewitness and participant, Joinville's account is of the first importance.

An English monk and chronicler, **Matthew Paris** (*c*.1200–59) wrote the *Chronica Majora*, a combination of his own work and that of Roger of Wendover. Paris's original contributions are much more in evidence after Wendover's death in 1235, and he offers useful insight into the political realities of the Latin East, in part through his friendship with Richard of Cornwall, who was an active participant in the Baron's Crusade of 1239–41. Paris is not always reliable and is partial to Emperor Frederick II and thus not necessarily even-handed with the Templars, with whom Frederick II had many a quarrel.

The **Munyatu ʾl-Guzāt** ('Wish of the Warriors of the Faith'), by an anonymous author, is a 14th-century 'Mamluk-Kipchak treatise on various aspects of *furūsiyya*' (Öztopçu 1986: xiii); written in Middle Turkic it is, like most *furūsiyya* literature, a copy of an earlier work on the same subject, the *Kitāb al-Furūsīyah wa-al-Baytarah* written by Muhammad ibn Yaʿqūb ibn Ghālib Ibn Akhī Hizām al-Khuttalī. It offers a complementary view to the work of al-ʾAqsarāʾī, reinforcing the view that horsemanship and archery were central to *mamlūk* warrior identity.

Oliver von Paderborn (*c*.1170–1227), teacher, preacher and crusader, was a participant in the venture into Egypt with his fellow Germans, and recorded what he saw of the campaign as it was happening in his book *Historia Damiatina* ('The History of Damietta'). His work, though a useful and usually accurate record of events, is seen through the eyes of a strongly religious man and as such victories and defeats tend to be, for Oliver, God-given in origin.

Roger of Wendover (d. 1236), an English monk and chronicler of the early and mid-13th century, wrote *Flores Historiarum* ('The Flowers of History'), a book that, like many of the period, was a conflation of the author's own works with those of others. Its value lies in the view it affords of contemporary European attitudes to the wars in the East and the enemy that was being fought there.

The **Rothelin Continuation** and **Eracles Continuation** were each a compilation of materials covering the history of the Latin East from the late 12th to the late 13th centuries. The *Eracles Continuation* covers the period from the 1180s up to 1275, while the *Rothelin Continuation* covers the period 1229 to 1261. Both were meant to be a continuation of William of Tyre's *Historia Hierosolymitana* ('The History of Jerusalem') which covered the period 1095–1184.

Modern sources

Addison, Charles Greenstreet (1842). *The History of the Knights Templars, the Temple Church, and the Temple*. London: Longman, Brown, Green, & Longmans.

al-Maqrīzī (1848). *Essulouk li Mariset il Muluk* ['The Road to Knowledge of the Return of Kings']. http://legacy.fordham.edu/halsall/source/makrisi.asp (accessed 1 June 2015).

Asbridge, Thomas (2011). *The Crusades: The Authoritative History of the War for the Holy Land*. London: HarperCollins.

Ayton, Andrew (1999). 'Arms, Armour, and Horses', in Maurice Keen, ed. *Medieval Warfare: A History*. Oxford: Oxford University Press, pp. 186–208.

Barber, Malcolm (1995). *The New Knighthood: A History of the Order of the Temple*. Cambridge: Canto.

Bennett, Matthew (1989). '*La Règle du Temple* as a Military Manual, or How to Deliver a Cavalry Charge', in C. Harper-Bill, C.J. Houldsworth & J.L. Nelson, eds. *Studies in Medieval History presented to R. Allen Brown*. Woodbridge: Boydell Press, pp. 7–19.

Budge, E.A. Wallis (1932). *The chronography of Gregory Abû'l-Faraj 1225-1286, the son of Aaron, the Hebrew physician commonly known as Bar Hebraeus, being the first part of his political history of the world*. Oxford: Oxford University Press. Excerpt, available online at: http://deremilitari.org/2014/01/the-seventh-crusade-1249-according-to-abu-al-faraj-gregory-bar-hebraeus/ (accessed 1 June 2015).

Cleve, Thomas C. van (1969). 'The Fifth Crusade', in *A History of the Crusades, Volume II. The Later Crusades, 1189–1311*. Madison, WI: University of Wisconsin Press, pp. 377–426.

Contamine, Philippe, trans. Michael Jones (1984). *War in the Middle Ages*. Oxford: Basil Blackwell (first published in French in 1980).

DeVries, Kelly (2002). *A Cumulative Bibliography of Medieval Military History and Technology (History of Warfare, Vol. 8)*. Leiden: Brill.

DeVries, Kelly, & Smith, Robert D. (2007). *Medieval Weapons. An Illustrated History of their Impact*. Santa Barbara, CA: ABC-CLIO.

Falk, Avner (2010). *Franks and Saracens. Reality and Fantasy in the Crusades*. London: Karnac Books.

Flori, Jean (2005). 'Ideology and motivations in the First Crusade', in Helen Nicholson, ed. *Palgrave Advances in the Crusades*. Basingstoke: Palgrave Macmillan, pp. 15–36.

France, John (1999). *Western Warfare in the Age of the Crusades, 1000–1300*. London: UCL Press

France, John (2005). 'Crusading Warfare', in Helen Nicholson, ed. *Palgrave Advances in the Crusades*. Basingstoke: Palgrave Macmillan, pp. 58–80.

Gabrieli, Francesco, ed. & Arabic trans. (2009). *Arab Historians of the Crusades*. Trans. from the Italian by E.J. Costello. London: Routledge (first published in English in 1969).

Hamblin, William J. (1992). 'Saladin and Muslim Military Theory', in Benjamin Z. Kedar, ed. *The Horns of Hattin*. Farnham: Variorum, pp. 228–38.

Hewitt, John (1996). *Ancient Armour & Weapons*. London: Random House (first published in 1855).

Hillenbrand, Carole (1999). *The Crusades: Islamic Perspectives (Islamic Surveys)*. Edinburgh: Edinburgh University Press.

Hillenbrand, Carole (2007). *Turkish Myth and Muslim Symbol: The Battle of Manzikert*. Edinburgh: Edinburgh University Press.

Hourani, Albert (2005). *A History of the Arab Peoples*. London: Faber and Faber (originally published in 1991).

Housley, Norman (2008). 'The thirteenth-century crusades in the Mediterranean', in *The New Cambridge Medieval History, Volume V, c.1198–c.1300*. Cambridge: Cambridge University Press, pp. 569–89.

Humphreys, R. Stephen (1977a). *From Saladin to the Mongols: The Ayyubids of Damascus, 1193–1260*. Albany, NY: State University of New York Press.

Humphreys, R. Stephen (1977b). 'The Emergence of the Mamluk Army', in *Studia Islamica*, Vol. XLV. Paris: Maisonneuve & Larose, pp. 67–99.

Humphreys, R. Stephen (1998). 'Ayyubids, Mamluks, and the Latin East in the 13th Century', in *Mamluk Studies Review*, Vol. II. Chicago, IL: Middle East Documentation Center, University of Chicago, 1–18. http://mamluk.uchicago.edu/MamlukStudiesReview_II_1998_18MB.pdf (accessed 1 June 2015).

Hyland, Ann (1996). *The Medieval Warhorse: From Byzantium to the Crusades*. Stroud: Sutton Publishing Ltd.

Irwin, Robert (2008). 'The Rise of the Mamluks', in *The New Cambridge Medieval History, Volume V, c.1198–c.1300*. Cambridge: Cambridge University Press, pp. 607–21.

Jensen, Kjersti Enger (2013). *The Mamluk Lancer. A philological study of Nihāyat al-su'l wa-'l-'umnīya fī ta'līm 'a'māl al-furūsīya*. MA thesis, University of Oslo.

Joinville, Jean de, trans. Sir Frank Marzials (1908). *Memoirs of the Crusades by Villehardouin and de Joinville*. London: J.M. Dent & Sons.

Jotischky, Andrew & Hull, Caroline (2005). *The Penguin Historical Atlas of the Medieval World*. London: Penguin.

Keen, Maurice (1990). *Chivalry*. New Haven, CT: Yale University Press (originally published in 1984).

Keen, Maurice, ed. (1999). *Medieval Warfare: A History*. Oxford: Oxford University Press.

Lev, Yaacov (1999). *Saladin in Egypt*. Leiden: Brill.

Levanoni, Amalia (2011). 'The *Halqah* in the Mamluk Army: Why Was It Not Dissolved When It Reached Its Nadir?', in *Mamluk Studies Review, Volume XV*. Chicago, IL: Middle East Documentation Center, University of Chicago, pp. 37–65. http://mamluk.uchicago.edu/MamlukStudiesReview_XV_2011.pdf (accessed 1 June 2015).

Lotan, Shlomo (2012). 'The Battle of La Forbie (1244) and its Aftermath – Re-examination of the Military Orders' Involvement in the Latin Kingdom of Jerusalem in the mid-Thirteenth Century', in *Ordines Militares Colloquia Torunensia Historica*, Vol. XVII, 53–67.

Maalouf, Amin, trans. Jon Rothschild (1984). *The Crusades through Arab Eyes*. London: Al Saqi Books.

Marshall, Christopher (1994). *Warfare in the Latin East, 1192–1291*. Cambridge: Cambridge University Press.

Marshall, Christopher J. (1990). 'The Use of the Charge in Battles in the Latin East, 1192–1291', in *Historical Research*, Vol. 63: 221–26.

Muldoon, James (2005). 'Crusading and canon law', in Helen Nicholson, ed. *Palgrave Advances in the Crusades*. Basingstoke: Palgrave Macmillan, pp. 37–57.

Nettles, Isolde Betty (2001). *Mamluk Cavalry Practices: Evolution and Influence*. PhD dissertation, University of Arizona.

Nicholson, Helen (2003). *Knight Templar 1120–1312*. Oxford: Osprey Publishing.

Nicholson, Helen (2004). *The Knights Templar: A New History*. Stroud: Sutton Publishing Ltd (first published in 2001).

Nicolle, David (1982). *The Military Technology of Classical Islam, Vols. 1–3*. Doctoral thesis, Edinburgh University. https://www.era.lib.ed.ac.uk/handle/1842/7432 (accessed 1 June 2015).

Nicolle, David (1993). *The Mamluks 1250–1517*. Oxford: Osprey Publishing.

Nicolle, David (1994). *Saracen Faris, AD 1050–1250*. Oxford: Osprey Publishing.

Nicolle, David (1996). *Knight of Outremer, 1187–1344 AD*. Oxford: Osprey Publishing.

Nicolle, David (1999a). *Arms and Armour of the Crusading Era, 1050–1350. Volume 1: Western Europe and the Crusader States*. London: Greenhill Books.

Nicolle, David (1999b). *Arms and Armour of the Crusading Era, 1050–1350. Volume 2: Islam, Eastern Europe and Asia*. London: Greenhill Books.

Nicolle, David (2011). *European Medieval Tactics (1): The Fall and Rise of Cavalry, 450–1260*. Oxford: Osprey Publishing.

Nicolle, David (2014). *Mamluk 'Askari, 1250–1517*. Oxford: Osprey Publishing.

Oakeshott, Ewart (2000). *Sword in Hand: A Brief History of the Knightly Sword*. Minneapolis, MN: Arms & Armor, Inc.

Öztopçu, Kurtuluş (1986). *A 14th Century Mamluk-Kipchak Military Treatise: Munyatu ' l-Guzāt*. PhD dissertation, University of California, Los Angeles.

Paris, A. (1871). *Chronique d'Ernoul et de Bernard le Trésorier*. Paris: Le Société de l'Histoire de France.

Paris, Matthew, trans. J.A. Giles (1852). *Matthew Paris's English History, from the Year 1235 to 1273, Volume 1*. London: Henry G. Bohn.

Peters, Edward (1971). *Christian Society and the Crusades, 1198–1229: Sources in Translation, Including 'The Capture of Damietta' by Oliver of Paderborn*. Philadelphia, PA: University of Pennsylvania Press.

Powell, James M. (1990). *Anatomy of a Crusade, 1213–1221*. Philadelphia, PA: University of Pennsylvania Press.

Runciman, Steven (1994). *A History of the Crusades, Volume III: The Kingdom of Acre and the Later Crusades*. London: The Folio Society (originally published in 1951).

Scanlon, George T., ed. & tr. (2012). *A Muslim manual of War, being Tafrij al-kurub fi tadbir al-hurub (The dispelling of woes in the management of wars)*. Cairo: The American University in Cairo Press (first published 1961).

Shirley, Janet (1999). *Crusader Syria in the Thirteenth Century: Rothelin Continuation of William of Tyre*. Farnham: Ashgate Publishing.

Smail, R.C. (1972). *Crusading Warfare, 1097–1193*. Cambridge: Cambridge University Press (first published in 1956).

Strayer, Joseph R. (1969). 'The Crusades of Louis IX', in *A History of the Crusades, Volume II. The Later Crusades, 1189–1311*. Madison, WI: University of Wisconsin Press, pp. 487–521.

Upton-Ward, Judith M. (2002). *The Rule of the Templars: The French Text of the Rule of the Order of Knights Templar*. Woodbridge: Boydell Press (first published in 1992).

Vitry, Jacques de (1896). *The History of Jerusalem*. London: Palestine Pilgrim's Text Society.

Wendover, Roger of, trans. C.D. Yonge (1853). *The flowers of History, especially such as relate to the affairs of Britain, from the beginning of the world to the year 1307, collected by Matthew of Westminster. Volume 2*. London: H.G. Bohn.

INDEX

References to images are shown in bold. References to plates are shown in bold with captions in parentheses.